DUNWOODIE

THE HEART OF THE CHURCH IN NEW YORK

Edited by
Deborah K. McCue

St. Joseph's Seminary   Yonkers, New York

On October 6th, 1995, His Holiness Pope John Paul II walked through the doors of the Saints Peter and Paul Chapel of St. Joseph's Seminary to pray with the seminary community. In his homily during the Vespers service the Holy Father delivered a *serious* message:

If you are to become priests, it will be for the purpose—above all other purposes—of proclaiming the word of God and feeding God's people with the body and blood of Christ. . . . If there is one challenge facing the Church and her priests today, it is the challenge of transmitting the Christian message whole and entire, without letting it be emptied of its substance. The Gospel cannot be reduced to mere human wisdom. Salvation lies not in clever human words or schemes, but in the cross and resurrection of our Lord Jesus Christ.

From the sanctuary of the one-hundred-year-old chapel, which has heard the prayers of over two thousand seminarians ordained to the priesthood, the Holy Father called the men of Dunwoodie his friends, and *friends can talk about serious matters.* His Holiness Pope John Paul II came to Dunwoodie to remind the seminarians: *The wisdom of the cross is at the heart of the life and ministry of every priest.* He came to Dunwoodie because it is "The Heart of the Church in New York."

Dunwoodie: The Heart of the Church in New York

Edited by Deborah K. McCue

Designed by Keith Lepkowski

All photography by Ani Antreasyan with the exception of the following:

Page 1: *St. Joseph's Seminary.* Photo: Chris Sheridan. Page 2: *Pope John Paul II at Dunwoodie.* Photo: L'Osservatore Romano. Page 11: *The Presentation of Jesus*, Dunwoodie, (detail on page 12). Photo: Gary Spector. Page 15: *Family Festival Day Recessional –Acolytes, Knights of Columbus, and Deacons.* Photo: Rev. James Hynes. Page 18: *Portrait of John Cardinal Farley*, Dunwoodie. Photo: Phil Persico. Page 19: *Portrait of Archbishop Michael A. Corrigan*, Dunwoodie. Photo: Phil Persico. *Dedication Day 1896*, Dunwoodie. Photo: Cathedral Library Association. Page 21: *Tomas Gonzalez and Family.* Photo: Phil Persico. Page 22: *Statue of St. Joseph*, Dunwoodie. Photo: Chris Sheridan. Page 23: *St. Joseph's Seminary*, 1896. Photo: Cathedral Library Association. Page 25: *The Lord's Supper*, Dunwoodie, (detail on page 26). Photo: Gary Spector. Page 38: *St. John's, Fordham, N.Y.* Photo: Cathedral Library Association. Page 40: *Dunwoodie Faculty, 1910.* Photo: source, *St. Joseph's Seminary, Dunwoodie, New York, 1896-1921*, by Rev. Arthur J. Scanlan. Page 41: *Centennial Year Faculty, 1996-1997.* Photo: Chris Sheridan. Page 44: *Class of 1900.* Photo: St. Joseph's Seminary. Page 45: *Seminarians, 1947.* Photo: St. Joseph's Seminary. Page 48: *Chapel of Mary Immaculate Seminary.* Photo: Luke Sweeney. Page 49: *William Schickel.* Photo: The Family of William Schickel. Page 50: *Class of 1997, Institute of Religious Studies.* Photo: © 1997 Barbara Hansen. Page 54: *Msgr. John M.A. Fearns with Msgr. Edward M. Betowski, 1952. Francis Cardinal Spellman Laying the Cornerstone of the Archbishop Corrigan Library, 1952.* Photos: St. Joseph's Seminary. Page 59: *The Agony in the Garden*, Dunwoodie, (detail on page 60). Photo: Gary Spector. Page 65: *Rev. Eric Raaser.* Photo: Archbishop Stepinac High School. Page 66: *Rev. S. Keith Outlaw.* Photo: Chris Sheridan. Page 67: *Msgr. John Carlin*, from his personal archives. Page 69: *Series of stained glass depicting the hands of a priest*, Dunwoodie. Photo: Phil Persico. Page 71: *SS. Peter and Paul Chapel Doors*, Dunwoodie, (detail on page 72). Photo: Gary Spector. Pages 72 and 73: *The Dome of St. Peter's Basilica.* Photo: Frank Bassett. Page 73: *Pope John Paul II, Feast of the Epiphany, 1997.* Photo: Patrick Byrne. Page 76. *Seminarians with Pope John Paul II, Centennial Pilgrimage, 1997.* Photo: L'Osservatore Romano. Page 77: *Centennial Pilgrims with Pope John Paul II, 1997.* Photo: Foto Felici. Page 79: *Seminarian James Vong, Siena.* Photo: Frank Bassett. Page 85: *The Crucifixion of Christ*, Dunwoodie, (detail on page 86). Photo: Gary Spector. Page 93: *The Resurrection of Christ*, Dunwoodie, (detail on page 94). Photo: Gary Spector. Page 98: *Ordination to a minor order, 1947.* Photo: St. Joseph's Seminary. Page 99: *SS. Peter and Paul Chapel, Golden Jubilee Year, 1947.* Photo: St. Joseph's Seminary. Page 100: *Portrait of Terence Cardinal Cooke*, Dunwoodie. Photo: Phil Persico. *Pope John Paul II praying in the SS. Peter and Paul Chapel*, Dunwoodie, 1995. Photo: L'Osservatore Romano. Page 101: *Altar Renovation*, 1983. Photo: St. Joseph's Seminary. *SS. Peter and Paul Chapel, Easter Vigil, 1997.* Photo: Msgr. Francis J. McAree. Page 104: *Donald Dumler.* Photo: Phil Persico. Page 105: *A Treasury of Sacred Music*, CD Cover Art. Graphic design and photo: Molly Ahearn.

Proofreading: Dr. Mary Ellen Hubbard, Katherine Krupp, and Rev. Edmund J. Whalen

Research assistance: Deacon Anthony P. Cassaneto, Trisha McMahon Drain, Rev. Msgr. Francis J. McAree, and Sr. Regina Melican

Production consultant: Steve Zane

Written contributions: B.C.—*Brian Caulfield* T.M.D.—*Trisha McMahon Drain* T.G.—*Tomas Gonzalez* G.H.—*George Hafemann* G.J.H.—*Gerard J. Hekker* M.E.H.—*Dr. Mary Ellen Hubbard* D.M.—*Deborah K. McCue* R.McK.—*Rev. Robert McKeon* R.M.—*Sister Regina Melican* W.B.S.—*Rev. Msgr. William B. Smith* E.W.—*Rev. Edmund Whalen* A.S.—*Rev. Anthony D. Sorgie* G.S.—*George Sears, Jr.*

The editor is grateful to Reverend Thomas J. Shelley for his work *Dunwoodie: The History of St. Joseph's Seminary, Yonkers, New York*, written at the request of His Eminence, John Cardinal O'Connor, Archbishop of New York, to commemorate the seminary's centenary. It has been a valuable resource in the preparation of this commemorative volume.

The publisher acknowledges the generous contribution of time and resources made by Carrafiello, Diehl, and Associates, Inc., of Irvington, New York, towards the production of this book.

ISBN 0-9659980-0-2

Library of Congress Catalog Card Number: 97-69520

Printed in the U.S.A. by Rosemont Press, Inc., New York, N.Y.

Acknowledgements

John Cardinal O'Connor
Archbishop of New York

Archbishop Edwin F. O'Brien
Archdiocese for Military Services, U.S.A.
former Rector of St. Joseph's Seminary

Reverend Anthony D. Sorgie
Vice Rector, St. Joseph's Seminary
Chairman, Exsultet! Easter Concert

Reverend Monsignor Francis J. McAree
Rector, St. Joseph's Seminary
Centennial Committee Chairman

Reverend Edmund J. Whalen
Vice-Rector, St. Joseph's Seminary
Chairman, Centennial Pilgrimage to Rome

Reverend Brian Barrett
Mr. John Hopkins
Chairmen, Family Festival Day

Reverend Monsignor Wallace Harris
Chairman, Alumni Day Mass and Dinner

Reverend Robert Robbins
Chairman, Centennial Dinner

Reverend Peter John Cameron, O.P.
Chairman, Academic Convocation

Reverend Robert McKeon
Chairman, Vocation Mass

Reverend Joseph R. Giandurco
Chairman, Centennial Mass,
St. Patrick's Cathedral

Excerpts from the following publications by St. Paul Books and Media are used with permission: *Constitution on the Sacred Liturgy, Sacrosanctum Concilium* © 1963, N.C.W.C. Bureau of Information translation; *Pastoral Constitution on the Church in the Modern World, Gaudium et Spes* © 1965, N.C.W.C. Translation; *Decree on the Apostolate of the Laity, Apostolicam Actuositatem* © 1965, N.C.W.C. Translation; *Decree on Priestly Training, Optatam Totius* © 1965, N.C.W.C. Translation; *I Will Give You Shepherds, Pastores Dabo Vobis* © 1992, Vatican Translation; *Tertio Millennio Adveniente* © 1994, Daughters of St. Paul. All rights reserved.

Scripture excerpts are taken from the *New American Bible* copyright © 1970 Confraternity of Christian Doctrine, Washington, D.C. Used with permission. All rights reserved.

Excerpts from the English translation of the *Ordination of Deacons, Priests, and Bishops* ©1975, International Committee on English in the Liturgy, Inc. (ICEL); excerpts from the English translation of *The Roman Missal* © 1973, 1985, ICEL. All rights reserved.

Excerpts from *Dunwoodie: The History of St. Joseph's Seminary, Yonkers, New York*, by Thomas J. Shelley © 1993, the Archdiocese of New York, are used with permission. All rights reserverd.

Excerpts from *St. Joseph's Seminary, Dunwoodie, New York, 1896-1921*, by Arthur J. Scanlan ©1922, the United States Catholic Historical Society. All rights reserved.

Excerpts from *The History of St. Joseph's Seminary of New York* © 1896, The Cathedral Library Association. All rights reserved.

"Prospects for Seminary Theology," by Reverend Avery Dulles, S.J., S.T.D., delivered September 17, 1997, at St. Joseph's Seminary, used with permission.

Articles by Brian Caulfield and Gerard J. Hekker as well as excerpts from Pope John Paul II's *Address to the Seminarians at Dunwoodie* first appeared in *Catholic New York* and are used with permission.

Detailed references can be found on page 116.

Dedicated to our brothers

Father Brian P. Barrett

and

Father Eugene R. Hamilton, Jr.

*You started this journey with us,
and we will end it with you,
as we follow in your footsteps. . .
from the garden of our Mother
into our Father's arms.*

TABLE OF CONTENTS

FOREWORD

O f all the many and varied institutions in the Church, that which is perhaps the most difficult to explain in a single volume is a seminary. Yet there is no institution more vital to the Church and more essential for Her future. Without priests, there is no Eucharist. Without the Eucharist, there is no Church. Priests, so much at the center of who we are as a Church, are formed in seminaries which, in the true sense of the word, educate the whole man so that he may give himself fully to God's people.

St. Joseph's Seminary, Dunwoodie, has served the Archdiocese of New York and numerous other dioceses and religious congregations since the closing years of the nineteenth century. As the twenty-first century dawns on the horizon, Dunwoodie instills in its students a deep love of the Church by combining the vitality of the Church's Tradition with insight into the needs of the modern world. Each seminarian is afforded a formation which enables him to be a priest ready to bring the light of the Gospel and the gift of the Eucharist to the Church in the New Millennium.

Similarly, the Permanent Diaconate Formation Program provides effective servants of the people of God whose ministry is invaluable in our parishes. The Institute of Religious Studies prepares religious and laity to be well-versed in the truth of the teaching of the Church so that they may build up in a multitude of ways the Body of Christ which is the Church.

As you read this volume and appreciate its beautiful photography, please remember to pray for the seminarians of St. Joseph's Seminary — the Priests of the New Millennium. They will be the ones to bring the Eucharist to the Church. Please God, they will be good priests, formed after the Heart of Christ, for they are formed at what is "The Heart of the Church in New York."

John Cardinal O'Connor
Archbishop of New York
July 1997

Facing page: John Cardinal O'Connor in the Basilica of SS. John and Paul, during the Centennial Pilgrimage, January 1997.

A very special responsibility falls upon the Christian family, which by virtue of the sacrament of matrimony shares in its own unique way in the educational mission of the Church — teacher and mother. As the synod fathers wrote: "The Christian family, which is truly a 'domestic church'..., has always offered and continues to offer favorable conditions for the birth of vocations."

POPE JOHN PAUL II

PASTORES DABO VOBIS

St. Joseph's Seminary Celebrates Family – "The First Seminary"

Archdiocesan Family Festival Day August 11, 1996

he first school every seminarian attends is Family School — the cradle of love and life. Seminary literally means "seed-bed." And priestly vocations are almost always first planted and nourished in the priest's own family.

In *Familiaris Consortio*, Pope John Paul II teaches that "the future of humanity passes by the way of the family"; so too does the future of the priesthood.

The family, the "domestic church," is the first school to convey life lessons about worthwhile values, serving brothers and sisters, fulfilling duties with generous fidelity, the first place to discover the Image of God in every brother and sister.

These life lessons are best and first learned at home and carry considerable influence on the formation of a future priest. The family setting a good example of domestic virtue can accompany the formative journey with prayer, respect, spiritual and material help, especially in difficult moments.

Pope John Paul II, addressing the

The Plan of Providence chose the priest's family to be the place in which his vocation was planted and nourished, an indispensable help for the growth and development of his vocation.

POPE JOHN PAUL II
PASTORES DABO VOBIS

Do not be afraid, I say, because great courage is required if we are to open the doors to Christ, if we are to let Christ enter into our hearts so fully that we can say with St. Paul, 'The life I live now is not my own: Christ is living in me.'

POPE JOHN PAUL II
ADDRESS AT DUNWOODIE

seminarians at Dunwoodie, urged them not to fear but to follow Christ closely, especially in a culture that flees from God and shows careless contempt for human life — that even in the face of a "culture of death" they be part of and contribute to a "culture of life." Every personal start in the "culture of life" begins in a person's own family where he first experiences how "to live in truth and in love."

In first celebrating the Family, Dunwoodie celebrates the obvious and the necessary. The seminary gratefully accepts their generous gifts, their sons, in order to form and return to the families of the dioceses it serves the gifts of priesthood — a generous exchange of gifts.

This seminary, any seminary, cannot forget from where it comes. Thus, our first acknowledgement is to thank the families who have given us their sons so that we in turn might serve the Family of Faith as faithfully as the faithful have served us.

— W.B.S.

Top: Second-year seminarian Brother Bernard Murphy, C.F.R., greets a young visitor at the beginning of a seminary tour.

Left: The Presentation of Jesus, detail from a stained glass window in the SS. Peter and Paul Chapel of St. Joseph's Seminary. The full window, seen on the previous page, is part of a series of windows in the chapel by Hardman of London, in which New Testament and Old Testament themes are paired to show that Christ brought to fulfillment that which had been promised. Here the Presentation of Jesus appears with the Sacrifice Offered by Abel.

You families and families like you have made the priesthood possible. These priests became priests because of your sacrifices and those of the broad family of the Church of New York.

CARDINAL JOHN O'CONNOR

JOHN CARDINAL O'CONNOR CELEBRATES THE FAMILY FESTIVAL DAY MASS

TO COMMEMORATE THE 100TH ANNIVERSARY OF THE DEDICATION OF ST. JOSEPH'S SEMINARY

On August 11, more than 4,000 parishioners from around the Archdiocese and beyond responded to the seminary's invitation to celebrate the family and the priesthood. Dunwoodie opened its doors and spacious 40 acres to the people who responded with gratitude and joy. Before the closing afternoon Mass, participants were treated to a day of sun, fun, food, games and prayer. A Sunday afternoon picnic atmosphere prevailed, with children the biggest winners. Countless seeds of vocations may have been planted as they kicked soccer balls, tossed basketballs and ran the relay races. The first Family Festival Day established a bond of love and support between the institution which prepares priests and the people who benefit from their ministry. Dunwoodie would no longer

be foreign ground for many.

The new bond was visible in the entrance procession of the closing Mass as the long line of priests wove through the crowd of thousands who showed their love and appreciation for the seminary and their priests by giving heartfelt greetings to Cardinal John O'Connor and the seventy-five priests in procession. Parishioners ran to photograph their pastors, parents shouldered their children for better views, waves and laughter were exchanged spontaneously. Both priests and people were blessed.

The cardinal delivered a strong message of hope for the future of the priesthood, and briefly summarized the seminary's one hundred years since its dedication on August 12, 1896.

This opening event of Dunwoodie's centennial celebration set the tone for the year to come. The message was clear that a priest must always work in relationship with God and His people, and the seminary was inviting the people to take an interest in and an ownership of the seminary—to share the joy of the priesthood. Thus, Family Festival Day fulfilled the seminary's centennial motto, "The Heart of the Church in New York." As Bishop Edwin F. O'Brien, Rector, explained, "The heart gives warmth and love. The mission of the priest is to bring life to the Church, and the love and warmth of Christ through the sacraments and pastoral care."

—B.C.

Top, left to right: Cardinal John O'Connor distributing communion; some of the 75 concelebrating priests; seminarians leading the recessional, followed by Fourth Degree Knights of Columbus and permanent deacons.

Bottom, left to right: Parishioners from St. John Vianney in the Bronx, wearing their distinctive purple tee-shirts; Father Anthony Sorgie, Professor of Sacred Music, conducting a choir of seminarians and lay people in the debut of the Mass composed by J. Michael Thompson in honor of the seminary's 100th anniversary; religious sisters enjoying the Mass; bringing up the gifts: three families from the parishes of St. Charles Borromeo, Skillman, N.J., St. Catherine's, Pelham, N.Y., and Our Lady of Fatima, Scarsdale, N.Y.

The ship of the Church is not sinking. We are battered but we are still here. The Church is still bringing forth apostles day after day. . . . The Gospel, the Good News, will be proclaimed day after day by your priests.

CARDINAL JOHN O'CONNOR

$\mathcal{W}$e have been blessed our entire lives by knowing such wonderful priests—all of whom came from this very seminary. We're so proud of all of them. This is their day. Why shouldn't we be here for them? Priests taught us, counselled us, comforted us, and guided us through life's tough decisions. They've been with us in our joys and heartbreaks. They married us, buried our dead, and have all the while been strong for us. Our priests have taught our children and have been terrific role models for us all. We're here at St. Joseph's because they are a big part of our lives. We love them and can't imagine going through life without their love and support.

CATHY ZSIDAY
ST. ELIZABETH ANN SETON PARISH
SHRUB OAK, NY

Clockwise, from top left:

Through seminari-an-led tours of Dunwoodie, its chapels, cloister, library and class-rooms . . .

Remembering the lives of the ordained alumni . . .

Celebrating the sacraments . . .

Through the eyes of a child . . .

And the sound of his drums . . .

A quiet "Ave" . . .

A joyous dance . . .

Diverse peoples gather together as the archdiocesan community cele-brates St. Joseph's Seminary and those who are called to serve.

An Archdiocese Rediscovers Its Seminary—

When St. Joseph's Seminary opened its doors to the greater Archdiocesan family, many people, for the first time, got a glimpse of what life is like for the seminarians studying here. Outside the entrance, a line formed for a guided tour which included the Romanesque Chapel of Saints Peter and Paul, made historic when Pope John Paul II celebrated Evening Prayer with the seminary community in 1995. Visitors were invited to walk through the recently installed doors bearing the words which mean so much to the Holy Father, *Aperite Portas Redemptori,* "Open the Doors to the Redeemer." Once inside they were treated to mini-recitals on the newly restored Casavant Frères organ while enjoying the beauty of the magnificent renovation of the icon of Christ Pantokrator which fills the apse and the words encircling the dome, *Tu es sacerdos in aeternum . . . ,* "You are a priest for ever . . . ."

While visitors enjoyed the art and architecture inside the seminary, others took advantage of the spiritual offerings outside. Sitting amongst the trees, priests quietly heard confessions. "Father," called a man from the path, "I've come all this way to see how you live. Are you ready to hear how I've lived? It's been years, Father. Do you have enough time for me?" The priest nodded, smiled and motioned to the man to take a seat.

For some, the day at the seminary was a day away from the harsh life of the city. A young man with a shoebox resting in his lap sat on a park bench in the shade of a giant elm, waiting for someone. "God is first, that's why I'm here. In the real world you don't see this type of atmosphere. Crime and drugs— that's what we're used to. It's so peaceful here, full of hope. This must be what heaven is like. I am waiting for the cardinal. I want him to bless my statue of Our Lady."

Back inside, visitors walked along the main hall where pictures of all the ordination classes are hung. They were all enjoying a game of "Find the Pastor." Two women huddled around one of these pictures. "I see a lot of happy faces in these pictures. They don't appear to be sacrificing anything. Instead they look like kids on Christmas morning. Children today need to know there is a lot of joy in serving God."

—T.M.D

And remembers when "Wisdom built herself a house" 100 years ago...

St. Joseph's Seminary Dedication Ceremony, August 12, 1896

At six o'clock on the morning of the twelfth, the day was begun by a proper and patriotic celebration on the lawn in front of the Seminary. A magnificent American flag, twenty by thirty feet in size . . . was blessed by the Rev. James N. Connolly . . . . Thus, under the protection of the great ensign, stands St. Joseph's Seminary . . . .

Promptly at ten o'clock the Archbishop, attended by Dean Lings of Yonkers and Dean Sweeney of Kingston, began the ceremony of the blessing of the new house of the Lord, and as the priests marched around in procession robed in cassock and surplice, they found the Chapel a fair and gladdening sight. . . . The sanctuary was a dream of golden glory . . . and the wondrous color harmonies of the stained glass windows sent a thrill of exultation through the souls of those who love and appreciate the glory of the house of God.

When the ceremony of the blessing was finished, the procession for the Solemn Pontifical Mass entered the Chapel. . . . More than two hundred priests occupied the stalls, with a few laymen invited as special guests by reason of their great interest in the building of the Seminary.

About twenty priests acted as a special choir, and sang the Gregorian Mass . . . .

—Excerpt from *The History of St. Joseph's Seminary in New York*, Cathedral Library Association

Excerpts from Bishop John Farley's Dedication Homily

When one tries to realize the condition of the Catholics of New York eighty years ago, when Bishop Connolly entered upon his episcopal office with two small churches all-sufficient for the total Catholic population of the city, with a few thousand souls scattered throughout the length and breadth of the States of New York and New Jersey, with scarcely a dozen priests to minister to the spiritual wants of all; when one contrasts that state of things with what we see around us today, one is forced to say, surely 'the finger of God is here. . . .'

It was a day full of hope and divinest promise when, five years ago, 100,000 of the faithful from all parts of this vast diocese, with their pastors at their head, at the invitation of their venerated Archbishop [John Cardinal McCloskey], gathered around this place to witness the planting of the tree under whose spreading shade we repose to-day, and of which for ages to come this diocese shall enjoy the consecrated fruit. . . .

The time had come for New York to have her own seminary within her own limit, as had originally intended by the former Bishops of the diocese; a

Your Grace [Archbishop Michael A. Corrigan], this must be for you one of the most consoling days of your life. . . . Your illustrious predecessors in this See sighed to behold this day; they saw it in spirit and were glad. They knew it would come, —that God would provide the means and the man. . . .

This latest and greatest gift of a grateful clergy and people, this future home of piety and learning, who can doubt, I say, that these holy patrons and prelates united their prayers and pleadings with those that fill your heart and the hearts of all the prelates and priests and people here to-day, that the Eternal Father would pour out upon this Seminary and upon all who shall dwell therein, the fulness of His blessing; that the Great High-Priest may make intercession for those who are to be made after His likeness here . . . that as generation after generation of young priests go forth from these sacred precincts, they may bear away with them the fulness of His wisdom and understanding, and counsel and fortitude, and knowledge, and piety and the fear of the Lord! That they may go and bring forth fruit, and that their fruit remain, to the honor and glory of God, to the salvation of souls, and to the lifting up of this our own beloved country to still higher planes of truth and honor and national prosperity.

seminary so placed that it should be under the eye and immediate guidance of the head of the diocese. That the time was ripe for it is evidenced by the marvellous success that has attended the work from the moment of its inception. That within five years from the laying of the first stone, 'this monumental structure, the most perfect model of its kind,' as Cardinal Ledochowski calls it truly, should have reached completion, with only such a residue of debt as a brief space will wipe out, truly is something without precedent in the Church of this country. . . .

Portraits from top left: John Cardinal Farley, Archbishop of New York , (1902-1918); Michael A. Corrigan, Archbishop of New York, (1885-1902), from St. Joseph's Seminary.

Right: Participants at the Dedication Day Ceremony, August 12, 1896. Archbishop Michael Corrigan is seated sixth from the left.

·One Hundred Years Later, Men Still

MY PARENTS' LOVE AND A LEAP OF FAITH
A Seminarian's Story

My parents' faith is one of the ways in which our Lord helped me and continues to help me strive towards giving myself completely to Him. They have always been there for me even when I did not realize it. My name is Tomas Gonzalez. I'm a young Hispanic-American from the upper part of Manhattan, and I am now in my first year of preparation towards the priesthood.

My parents' simple witness of love and sacrifice helped me to embrace this call to enter the seminary. They taught me how to pray by leading me and my sisters in pray-

ing a family rosary and showing us their love of God through their involvement in the Church and their love for one another, so very evident wherever they go. This love is contagious and continues to assist me in finding the courage I need to sustain my desire to become a priest for Jesus Christ.

My parents' tireless efforts have revealed to me that they are living instruments of God, reflecting the words Pope John Paul II has stressed to the youth of the world during his pontificate—"Be not afraid." These words go straight to the human heart. I have come to understand what they mean by facing my own fear of commitment. At times, doubtful thoughts suddenly overwhelmed me and I wondered if my desire

...A Journey Which, For

I appeal especially to families. May parents, mothers in particular, be generous in giving their sons to the Lord when he calls them to the priesthood. May they cooperate joyfully in their vocational journey, realizing that in this way they will be increasing and deepening their Christian fruitfulness in the Church. . . .

POPE JOHN PAUL II
PASTORES DABO VOBIS

Follow Their Hearts to Dunwoodie...

to become a priest was really only an emotional response to an overzealous involvement with prayer and church activities. But I learned the doubts were really a fear of giving my life to God, and this in turn showed me the way to learn how to trust Him and believe that He would not call me to a life that I could not live, for with Him, *all is possible.*

I believe that God will assist all those who surrender themselves to Him so that His love may spread to all mankind. But first one must trust Him, confront fears, and with courage, take the *leap of faith.* This is what I have learned from my parents.

—T.G.

Top: First-year seminarian Tomas Gonzalez with his family.

Left: Seminarians: Brother Richard Roemer, C.F.R., Deacon Richard D. Smith, and Floyd Grace.

Many, Began at Home

On the Eve of the Millennium, St. Joseph's Seminary Continues its Mission to Serve the Families of the Archdiocese of New York

I say . . .
with all my heart,
to the new St. Joseph's,
ESTO PERPETUA!

BISHOP HENRY GABRIELS
OF OGDENSBURG,
ON THE OCCASION
OF THE DEDICATION OF
ST. JOSEPH'S SEMINARY

The future is never altogether different from the past. One hundred years ago Dunwoodie was conceived and born into a world that was already experiencing unprecedented change. In lecture halls and in learned journals distinguished scholars were questioning the very foundations of the Christian faith and posing a daunting intellectual challenge . . . . At the same time the ferry boats from Ellis Island were daily disgorging thousands of poor immigrants who threatened to overwhelm the pastoral resources of the archdiocese.

Today the secularization of American culture continues unabated and the Catholic church in the United States—especially in the Archdiocese of New York—remains more than ever the immigrant church. All that has changed is the place of origin of the immigrants. A century ago the priests of New York struggled to provide for the pastoral needs of the Irish and the Germans, the Slavs, and the Italians. Today they need to offer comparable service to the Blacks and Hispanics, Haitians and Asians, and all the varied peoples who constitute the polyglot population of the archdiocese.

A century ago Dunwoodie prepared its students to meet the challenges of that day by offering them an intellectual and spiritual formation that drew its inspiration from both "the ancient faith and modern thought." As Dunwoodie begins its second century of service to the people of New York, it need only look to its own proud history for guidance and direction.

—Reverend Thomas J. Shelley, Professor of History,
from *Dunwoodie: The History of St. Joseph's Seminary*

1840 Bishop John Hughes established the first St. Joseph's Seminary at Fordham in the Bronx.

1864 - New York diocesan priests were trained at St. Joseph's Provincial
1896 Seminary in Troy, New York.

1886 Archbishop Michael Augustine Corrigan announced his intention of providing New York with a modern seminary facility.

1890 The Valentine Estate in Dunwoodie, Yonkers, was purchased.

1891 May 17, the cornerstone was blessed. Construction began later that same year.

1896 August 12, the building was dedicated. The seminary opened its doors in September of that year.

1900 April 19, Archbishop Michael A. Corrigan consecrated the seminary chapel, his gift to St. Joseph's.

1941 May 14, the 25th anniversary of his ordination to the priesthood, Francis Cardinal Spellman celebrated Mass in the seminary chapel and announced plans to construct a new gymnasium and infirmary.

1945- St. Joseph's Renaissance - Cardinal Spellman invested over
1967 $4,000,000 in renovations that included new furniture, painting, rewiring, redecoration of the chapel and the construction of a new library and gymnasium.

1952 October 29, Cardinal Spellman blessed the cornerstone for the new Corrigan Memorial Library.

1953 October 4, the new library was dedicated.

1967 May 11, the Cardinal Spellman Recreation Building was dedicated.

1983 Terence Cardinal Cooke restored the main chapel of Dunwoodie, the Chapel of Saints Peter and Paul.

1995 October 6th, Pope John Paul II celebrated Vespers with the seminary community and dedicated the new chapel doors bearing the words which inaugurated his pontificate, *Aperite portas Redemptori*, "Open the doors to the Redeemer."

Never before had the archdiocese incurred such a huge debt or paid it off so quickly. What made the achievement all the more remarkable was that the bulk of the money came from the modest donations of hundreds of thousands of ordinary working people.

REVEREND THOMAS J. SHELLEY,
DUNWOODIE: THE HISTORY OF ST. JOSEPH'S SEMINARY

The "seminary" . . . more than a place, a material space, should be a spiritual place, a way of life, an atmosphere that fosters and ensures a process of formation, so that the person who is called to the priesthood by God may become, with the sacrament of orders, a living image of Jesus Christ, head and shepherd of the Church.

POPE JOHN PAUL II
PASTORES DABO VOBIS

ST. JOSEPH'S SEMINARY MAKING TRUE SHEPHERDS OF SOULS

CENTENNIAL ACADEMIC CONVOCATION SEPTEMBER 17, 1996

 he Mission of St. Joseph's Seminary and College as the major seminary of the Archdiocese of New York is carried out in four distinct ways.

The primary mission is to achieve excellence in priestly formation for candidates to the Roman Catholic priesthood by providing:

• a comprehensive program of human, spiritual, intellectual, and pastoral formation designed to enable the seminarians to prepare for the ordained priesthood with a clear sense of priestly identity. This includes the understanding, as Second Vatican Council teaches, that the ministerial priesthood differs in essence from the priesthood of the baptized. "Seminarians presented for priestly ordination should be converted to the service of Christ, understand the tradition of the Church, and possess the attitudes and skills necessary to begin the priestly ministry" (PPF, 249).

• a Master of Divinity program dedicated to academic excellence and professional competence for seminarians. Students

The Seminary . . . is above all an educational community in progress . . . established by the bishop to offer those called by the Lord to serve as Apostles the possibility of re-living the experience of formation which our Lord provided for the Twelve.

POPE JOHN PAUL II
PASTORES DABO VOBIS

enrolled in this program also receive the degree of Bachelor of Sacred Theology, awarded through the Pontifical University of St. Thomas Aquinas in Rome.

• a Master of Arts program to provide an advanced degree in Theology.

A second aspect of the mission is to provide a spiritual, theological, and pastoral formation program for candidates preparing for the Permanent Diaconate.

A third aspect is to provide a program of studies faithful to the magisterium of the Church to serve as a preparation or ongoing education for those involved in the work of the Church and a means of doctrinal formation for those laity who desire to live their faith more fully. To this end the Seminary offers a Master of Arts in Religious Studies, granted through the Institute of Religious Studies, to any qualified student, lay, religious or clergy.

A fourth aspect is to provide consultation and resources for the Archdiocese of New York.

—from *St. Joseph's Seminary School of Theology Centennial Year Bulletin*

As this evening's convocation heralds the accomplishments of a century past, may it ignite dreams for another century to come. Your presence among us, representatives of church and state, religious communities and learned societies, seminaries and educational institutions of every level, Catholic faithful and other believers; your presence comes at some sacrifice for many. It reminds us that dreams of the future to be realized require no less the prayer, and the labor and the collaboration that have proved so essential for our past century's accomplishments. I welcome you with heartfelt gratitude for the encouragement your presence brings and with the request that you continue to encourage and embolden us toward a future of dedicated sacrifice for the building up of our church, and for the wonderfully diverse families of peoples she seeks to serve.

BISHOP EDWIN F. O'BRIEN
RECTOR OF DUNWOODIE, OPENING REMARKS DURING
THE ACADEMIC CONVOCATION

A century of marvelous achievement, training more than 2,000 men for the holy priesthood.
BISHOP PATRICK J. SHERIDAN
ACADEMIC CONVOCATION

Far left: The Lord's Supper, detail from a stained glass window in the main chapel, Dunwoodie. The full window, seen on the previous page is paired with the Old Testament's First Passover Meal in Egypt.

Left: Bishop Edwin F. O'Brien, Rector.

Academic Convocation 1996

A GATHERING TO RECOGNIZE THE
PURSUIT OF ACADEMIC EXCELLENCE
AT ST. JOSEPH'S SEMINARY

*This page, left to right:
Faculty and bishops share
the speakers' platform at
the Academic Convocation.*

*Representatives from
Colleges and Universities:
the Very Reverend
John P. McGuire, O.P.,
S.T.D., Reverend
Monsignor Thomas
Bergin, M.A. and the
Very Reverend Gerald L.
Brown, S.S., Ph.D.*

*Opposite page, top right:
Archbishop Daniel
Buechlein of Indianapolis
representing the
National Catholic
Conference of Bishops.*

On Tuesday evening, September 17, 1996, an impressive assemblage of delegates from colleges, universities, and learned societies, as well as faculty past and present, alumni and students, donned caps, gowns, and academic hoods for the procession into the Cardinal Spellman Recreation Center, transformed into a panoply of color and pageantry thanks to the efforts of convocation organizer Father Peter John Cameron, O.P., M.F.A., S.T.L., Dunwoodie's Professor of Homiletics. This diverse group of over 350 men and women, clergy, lay and religious, came together to affirm their faith, educational vocation and support of St. Joseph's Seminary. John Cardinal O'Connor, last to join in the procession, paused briefly to brush his hand over the door jamb before entering the auditorium. This meditative gesture anticipated his words spoken later in the evening, when the Cardinal shared his hopes for Dunwoodie's second hundred years and the men who will come from "our Catholic homes" through the doors of St. Joseph's into the bright future of the priesthood.

The highlight of the convocation was a

thought-provoking address by the Reverend Avery Dulles, S.J., S.T.D., the scholar-in-residence at Dunwoodie for the 1996–1997 academic year. The role of the seminary as the locus where rigorous academics, pastoral sensitivity, and spiritual insight meet was at the core of Fr. Dulles' challenge to St. Joseph's Seminary to fulfill the title "The Heart of the Church in New York." The role of the seminary as the conserver of the truth of theological reflection within the context of the magisterium was a consistent theme in the address. Fr. Dulles admitted that the university and seminary take different approaches to the study of theology. At the same time, he called for a mutual understanding between the two institutions with the result that theological study is enriched in both settings.

A reception in the seminary refectory followed the convocation. Guests enjoying the seminary's hospitality had time to share some thoughts about the importance of Dunwoodie. Monsignor Thomas J. Bergin, M.A., Vicar for Education in the Archdiocese of New York observed, "Academics are important, but St. Joseph's

recognizes the need that God wants priests who, yes, are smart—and that includes being street smart—but also having spiritual light and soul. In many ways, you're standing in the heart of the Church in New York, the gem of our educational system." Father Mark Vaillancourt of St. Charles Church on Staten Island explained, "We're here today for the good of St. Joseph's and for the good of the priesthood. It is important to make the connection between intellectual life and the priesthood."

Among those attending this celebration were lay students from the seminary's Institute of Religious Studies, founded in 1977. Susan Cosby, a physical therapist completing her final semester in the Institute's M.A. program, called the Institute "the best kept secret of the Archdiocese." Ms. Cosby applauded the seminary's efforts to educate lay people so that they can enrich their own faith and better serve their parishes.

—R.G & T.M.D.

PROSPECTS FOR SEMINARY THEOLOGY

CONVOCATION ADDRESS
SEPTEMBER 17, 1996

CENTENNIAL YEAR
SCHOLAR-IN-RESIDENCE
REVEREND AVERY DULLES, S.J., S.T.D.
LAURENCE J. MCGINLEY PROFESSOR,
FORDHAM UNIVERSITY

The Varieties of Theology

Christian theology takes on many different hues depending to some extent on the environment in which it is conducted. In the first few centuries theology was closely bound up with the catechetical school and with the cathedral chair from which the bishop preached to catechumens and to his flock. The theology of the day had strong apologetic and liturgical dimensions. In the early Middle Ages it took on a more contemplative character. Seeking to grow in holiness, the monks meditated in chapel or in their cells on the Word of God that had been read to them from the pulpit. In the high Middle Ages theology became more dialectical and scholastic; it was taught as a speculative science from the *cathedra* of the professor on the basis of authoritative texts. After the Council of Trent in the sixteenth century, the primary locus of theology, in many Catholic countries, moved to the seminaries and houses of formation of religious orders. It was oriented to the defense of the true faith and the refutation of insurgent heresies. In recent years an increasing proportion of North American theology is being done in centers and institutes that are intended, in many cases, to promote a Christian vision of society. In the Third World, liberation theology has grown in great part out of the concerns of the poor in basic Christian communities. In the past generation there has also been an increase of free-lance journalistic theology.

University Theology

For purposes of this lecture it may suffice to concentrate on the two principal arenas of theology in the United States today. They are, I believe, the university and the seminary. In the typical American university, theology has clearly lost its medieval status as "queen of the sciences." Our universities have been constructed on the model of University of Berlin in the early nineteenth century. The university is considered a place in which research is carried on according to the principles of scientific method, beginning with hard data of positive science and facts that can be recognized by any normal person. Thanks to the ingenuity of Friedrich Schleiermacher, theology managed to find a place in the secular university, but only as a professional school, parallel to other learned professions such as law and medicine. The aim of theology, in liberal Protestantism, was the training of the clergy. For this reason divinity schools hold only a marginal place in most nondenominational universities. Within the university, the study of religion is tolerated, provided that it is conducted on objective scientific principles and detaches itself from any particular faith-commitment.

In the typical American Catholic university theology has a more secure place, but is still seeking to define itself. In the past fifty years or so, some study of theology is normally required of undergraduates. A few universities have graduate departments of theology which are aimed primarily at the training of future teachers of religion or theology. Instead of being housed in a divinity school, theology is carried on predominantly in the school of arts and sciences. It has the status of a department, parallel to classics or mathematics. Degrees in theology are awarded according to standards already established for the bachelor's, master's or doctor's degree in other academic disciplines.

In the typical American university, whether or not it be Catholic, no ecclesiastical authority has direct control over the faculty of theology. As a department it is headed by a chairperson who reports to the dean of arts and sciences, to the faculty senate, and to the academic vice president. The university situation puts pressure on theology to present itself as a fully scientific discipline, open to critical inquiry. The principles of academic freedom recognized in American higher education are seen as exempting university theology from any

> *If the law of prayer establishes the law of belief, as the ancient adage has it, theology can only rise to its full stature when practiced in a community of prayer.*
>
> FR. AVERY DULLES

ecclesiastical control. Decisions with regard to hiring, promotion, and tenure of faculty are commonly reached on the basis of scholarly publications and teaching performance, without regard for the candidate's religious affiliation, convictions, and practice. Faculty and students are not presumed to be Catholic or even Christian. They may belong to any religion or none. Anything savoring of indoctrination in the classroom is disavowed. Course descriptions sometimes describe theology as being aimed to induce the students to think critically about any and all church traditions.

It so happens, in many cases, that teachers of theology do communicate faith and orthodox teaching, but the opposite can also happen. A tenured professor who diverges from Church teaching, even to the extent of becoming an agnostic or an atheist, will probably not be dismissed. A multitude of financial and legal pressures, as well as the university's commitment to academic freedom and autonomy, militate against penalizing any faculty member for lack of doctrinal orthodoxy.

Problematic Features

The university situation offers advantages and disadvantages. The opportunities for dialogue with other disciplines and for scholarly research are clear assets. Responding to the challenge of alien systems of thought, nineteenth-century university theologians such as Johann Sebastian von Drey, Johan Adam Möhler, John Henry Newman, and Maurice

Blondel made creative contributions that have advanced Catholic thinking on various fronts, but other university theologians such as Georg Hermes, Anton Günther, Ignaz Döllinger, and Alfred Loisy yielded too much ground to the demands of scientific rationality and fell into doctrinal errors.

This mixed record has continued in the twentieth century. During the first World War Karl Barth protested that German university theology had falsified the gospel by identifying itself too closely with the prevailing national culture. On the eve of the second World War theologians of the stature of Heinrich Schlier and Dietrich Bonhoeffer resigned their professorships and protested that theology must remain in the hands of the church, to which the Word of God had been entrusted.[1] Schlier was soon to become a Roman Catholic. Bonhoeffer, after resigning from the University of Berlin in 1935, founded a religious community for seminarians and newly ordained priests. Explaining his motives, he wrote to a friend: "The whole ministerial education today belongs to the Church—monastic-like schools in which pure doctrine, the Sermon on the Mount, and liturgy are taken seriously. In the university all three are not taken seriously, and it is impossible to do so under present circumstances."[2]

Like these Lutheran theologians, Catholics commonly recognize that Catholic theology must always be a reflection on the faith of the Church, practiced within the community of faith, with a view to serv-

ing and enhancing the spiritual life of that community. If it detaches itself from the Church and makes itself accountable to some other public, such as the state or the academy, it denatures itself as theology. The Congregation of the Doctrine of the Faith, in its instruction, "On the Ecclesial Vocation of the Theologian,"[3] has clarified these points.

The Seminary: Doctrinal Purity

This finding brings me to the main topic of the present address: seminary theology. The seminary, I shall contend, offers strengths precisely at those points where university theology is most precarious. Conducted within the Church in monastic-like communities, it stands firmly on the three pillars noted by Bonheoffer: pure doctrine, evangelical spirituality, and liturgical piety.

With regard to doctrine, the Catholic Church is committed to the view that faith is not simply a private disposition of soul. The faith has public manifestations: it has been expressed in the form of doctrines revealed by God and certified by Holy Scripture, tradition, and the magisterium. A major task of theology is to identify these truths, to defend them, and to explore their implications. Because the seminary operates under the direct authority of the bishop or bishops, and because it seeks to prepare priests who will nourish the people with the food of God's word, the seminary is alert to prevent the truths of faith from being ignored or denied, as sometimes happens in universities.

The Curriculum

In speaking of pure doctrine, Bonhoeffer's first requirement, one must consider the curriculum. The candidate for the priesthood, according to John Paul II, must be led "to a complete and unified vision of the truths which God has revealed in Jesus Christ . . . . Hence the need to know 'all' the Christian truths, without arbitrarily selecting among them, and to know them in an orderly fashion."[4] Seminary students are not admitted to the theology program without an impressive preparation in philosophy, spirituality, and preseminary theology. Then they normally spend some four years on intensive course work in which they do extensive exegesis of the Old and New Testaments, survey the entire history of the Church, and familiarize themselves with the whole body of Christian doctrine, not to mention their formation in pastoral skills, such as liturgy, homiletics, and canon law.[5] The full coverage of doctrine in the usual seminary course compares favorably with the rather selective exposure to doctrine in many university graduate programs, even on the doctoral level.

To enter into the M.A. program here at Dunwoodie one must have already completed the six semesters of the M.Div. program, whereas a university M.A. in theology requires only an undergraduate training in theology. By the time that one obtains the M.A. here at Dunwoodie one must have completed more than one hundred credits in graduate theology, whereas at a typical Catholic university such as Fordham some thirty credit hours are sufficient. In terms of hours of instruction the typical seminarian has much more to show than the university graduate student.

Equally important is the integration of doctrine in terms of the great mystery of God's self-communication in Christ and the Holy Spirit. No fragmentation of the curriculum is tolerated. According to the *Program of Priestly Formation* drawn up by the National Conference of Catholic Bishops in 1992, "the sacred sciences must themselves be taught as parts of a larger undertaking in which the whole—the Gospel—precedes and encompasses the parts."[6] Faculty and students in the seminary are committed to the belief that God has definitively revealed Himself in Christ, the divine Teacher who animates and guides the Church by the Holy Spirit. The same cannot always be said of theology departments in Catholic universities.

The Spiritual Dimension

Seminary theology benefits, furthermore, from Bonhoeffer's second requirement. The spirituality of the Gospel and of the Sermon on the Mount is taken with utmost seriousness. The Church intends to ordain to the priesthood only those who have been called by the Lord; in the program of formation it seeks to develop in the seminarians what John Paul II calls "a conscious and free response of adherence and involvement of their whole person with Jesus Christ, who calls them to intimacy of life with him and to share in his mission of salvation."[7] Every seminarian is expected to be pursuing an assiduous life of prayer under the guidance of competent spiritual directors. As Vatican II declared in its *Decree on Priestly Formation*, students of theology "should be trained for the ministry of the word so that they may gain an ever-increasing understanding of the revealed word of God, making it their own by meditation and giving it expression in their speech and in their lives. . . . Those who are to be configured to Christ the Priest through sacred ordination should form the habit of drawing close to him as friends in every detail of their lives" (OT 4 and 8).

This spiritual formation is not a distraction from theology, but a singular help for it. If the law of prayer establishes the law of belief, as the ancient adage has it, theology can only rise to its full stature when practiced in a community of prayer. Pope John Paul II asserts as much in his exhortation on priestly formation: "To be pastorally effective, intellectual formation is to be integrated with a spirituality marked by a personal experience of God. In this way a purely abstract approach to knowledge is overcome in favor of that intelligence of heart which knows how 'to look beyond,' and then is in a position to communicate the mystery of God to the people."[8]

An authentic life of prayer protects theology from the danger of being a mere memory lesson. As a contemporary Protestant theologian puts it: "Theological appraisal inevitably must formulate the tradition in such a way that its enduring references are uncovered and grasped as real and true. This goes beyond historical knowledge of ecclesial existence to the discernment of truth, its disclosive character, its enduring illuminative power."[9] Theology, rightly practiced, is a great intellectual adventure, in which the mind is plunged ever more deeply into the mysterious truth of revelation. It enables the student to put on the mind of Christ the eternal Teacher, who is the light of the world, and to see reality, as it were, through his eyes. By the gift of the Holy Spirit human beings can in faith rise to contemplate and savor the mystery of God's design.[10]

The Liturgical Dimension

The final characteristic of seminary theology, as described by Bonhoeffer, is its connection with worship. The subject matter of theology requires students who are capable of apprehending God in those places where he is pleased to make himself present.[11] According to Catholic faith God is really present in the Church's worship, in the sacraments, and supremely, in the Eucharist. By full, conscious, and active participation in sacramental celebrations the seminarian, like others, may attain those dispositions of gratitude, self-offering, and charity that will open his eyes to the presence of Christ in other persons and in the events of the day. Inasmuch as the sacraments are living actions of Christ in his Church, sacramental participation is an indispensable aid for building up an authentically Catholic sense of the faith.

The university department cannot normally provide a suitable setting for liturgy, but the Catholic seminary is by its nature a worshipping community. The community is molded daily through meditation on the word of God and through the celebration of the Eucharist, whereby the students are inserted in a living way into the Paschal mystery that they are studying in the classroom.[12] The seminary community is expected to be ecclesial, not simply because it is preparing celebrants of future parish liturgies but because the grace of the sacraments sustains the whole course of theological formation. As John Paul II explains in his exhortation on priestly formation: "In its deepest identity the seminary is called to be, in its own way, a continuation in the Church of the apostolic community gathered about Jesus, listening to his word, proceeding toward the Easter experience, awaiting the gift of the Spirit for the mission."[13]

Limitations

Having surveyed many assets of seminary theology, we may now turn to consider its possible and actual limitations. Seminary theology must be recognized as only one species: it cannot aspire to encompass the whole field of theology. By its very nature, it concentrates on those aspects that are particularly pertinent to the formation of future priests, who must be equipped to serve as ministers of word and sacrament and as pastoral leaders. The seminary cannot give equal attention to issues that do not enter into the normal scope of parish duties. The special questions that arise in the various sciences and professions, includ-

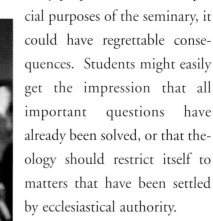

ing the worlds of business and finance, must be dealt with by other agencies.

Because of its specific finality, seminary formation must strive to impart the heritage of faith as already accessible through Scripture, tradition, and the teaching of the ecclesiastical magisterium. The typical seminary does not engage deeply in the exploration of new and difficult questions, to which no assured answers have as yet been given. While this orientation is entirely proper in view of the special purposes of the seminary, it could have regrettable consequences. Students might easily get the impression that all important questions have already been solved, or that theology should restrict itself to matters that have been settled by ecclesiastical authority.

Anti-intellectualism has often been characterized as an American disease, and regrettably our Catholic clergy have no immunity against it. In their zeal to impart sound doctrine, the faculty could implant a lack of appreciation for serious thinkers who are grappling with unresolved questions. The rapid developments in science and technology that are occurring in our day pose moral and doctrinal problems that demand careful study, patient dialogue and, in many cases, tentative answers. When such questions arise, it is not enough for theologians to appeal to Rome for an authoritative answer. Some responsible input should be offered by the theologians of the region from which the questions come. The priest, even if he is not competent to contribute to the discussion of these issues, should show respect and understanding for those who are so engaged.

Concerned to inculcate permanent and unalterable truths in the minds of their students, some professors overlook the kind of doctrinal development that John Henry Newman so brilliantly explained in his classic work on the subject. They give the impression that what is taught today was always the formulated doctrine of the Church. Others, seeking to be contemporary, fall victim to transitory fads and fashions. In either case, the effects are unfortunate. Priests who were formed in "non-historical orthodoxy" have no way of dealing with change, when it comes about. And those whose formation was too trendy are no better off. The priests of my generation were rather narrowly formed in a vintage of neoscholasticism that has practically died out since Vatican II. Some of them were paralyzed by the changes of the 1960s. I worry that priests who are too exclusively trained in current historical-critical approaches to Scripture or in the social analysis of liberation theology may find themselves in a similar situation when these trends go out of fashion. By immersing themselves in the long history of dogma, they can come to understand how the Church adapts its tradition to meet new threats and new opportunities as they arise.

I have heard the complaint, at least in some seminaries, that with the long hours spent in the classroom and with the constant encroachment of practical courses and field work, the students are given too little time for reading and reflection. It is not enough for them to learn by rote the answers given in textbooks or professor's notes. In their formational years they must acquire the habit of keeping up with current literature, including the more recent pronouncements from the Holy See. Professionals in every field are required to keep abreast of new developments in their field under pain of losing their qualifications to practice. The ministry should be no exception. The ideal would be to inoculate the students with what James Bryant Conant once called "the virus of self-perpetuating education."[14] A good education, I believe, can never be a terminal one.

Growth Toward the Future

For greater vitality of seminary theology and for the service of the local church, it may be hoped that some of the larger seminaries will develop graduate faculties and run regular sabbatical programs and institutes for the continuing education of the clergy. Pope John Paul II devotes an entire chapter of his exhortation on priestly formation to this theme. "The idea that priestly formation ends on the day one leaves the seminary," he declares, "is false and dangerous."[15] I am aware that St. Joseph's Seminary already does a great deal for continuing education. In the future it could perhaps develop a large component that would be engaged in research, reflection, and publication on current problems, such as inculturation and evangelization, thus offering stimulation and guidance for archdiocesan offices and programs. In this way this seminary could become more visible as a theological power-house and could more amply deserve the title already bestowed upon it in the motto of this centennial year: "the heart of the Church in New York."

The mission of a prominent seminary such as this should not be restricted to the archdiocese. If my analysis of the theological situation is accurate, seminaries are today being called to take on a greater share of responsibility for the future of the theological enterprise on the national and international scene. It may be necessary to release more priests for graduate study and to expand the seminary faculty so that its members have more time for research and publication. To assume the leadership to which they are called, seminary professors may have to publish more books, write more frequently for opinion-making journals, give more major addresses at theological conventions, and be more heavily involved in theological commissions and ecumenical and interreligious dialogues. Otherwise creative theologians may be tempted to move from the seminaries to the universities. The relatively low visibility of seminary professors who stand firmly within the Catholic tradition allows more adventurous university professors to steal the limelight, thus contributing to the false impression that theology is most vital when it liberates itself from its ecclesial matrix.

It is often said that in the past fifty years the center of theological activity has moved from the seminary to the university.[16] In view of the current prob-

> *It is often said that in the past fifty years the center of theological activity has moved from the seminary to the university. . . . To avoid chaos in their discipline university faculties must find ways of integrating their theology more successfully into the life and mission of the Church.*
>
> FR. AVERY DULLES

lems of university theology, this shift may not be entirely for the better. To avoid chaos in their discipline university faculties must find ways of integrating their theology more successfully into the life and mission of the Church. Unless they can do so, the hegemony may revert once more from the universities to seminaries and monasteries, where greater attention is paid to "pure doctrine, the Sermon on the Mount, and the liturgy."

In the present situation one may hope for a more vital interaction between the two types of institution. The seminary, as it typically exists today, relies on university theologians to address new and complex questions and to engage in creative research. The university, conversely, needs the seminary to maintain a deeper ecclesial sense and a firmer pastoral commitment. Faculties of both types can assist one another. The fact that I, as a university professor, have been invited to be a scholar-in-residence at this seminary in this centenary year, and to give the present convocation address, may be a signal that the gulf between the two types of institutions is narrowing, to the enrichment of both.

—*See page 116 for author's notes.*

Photos in this section: Father Avery Dulles; Cardinal John O'Connor and Bishop Edwin F. O'Brien; at prayer in the choir loft; distributing communion; Father Romanus Cessario, O.P., delegate from St. John's Seminary, Brighton, Massachusetts; Father Edmund J. Whalen, S.T.D., teaching a class in moral theology.

BEGINNINGS

BEFORE DUNWOODIE

Nyack on the Hudson River (1833–34)

At the time when Bishop John Dubois decided to build the first New York Seminary, there were nine churches, twenty-four priests and 150,000 Catholics in the diocese. His letter to the Association of Lyons, dated March 16, 1830, voiced his intentions:

Before all I must establish an apostolic nursery . . . . My idea is to unite a college with the seminary, as I did so happily in the Baltimore diocese [Mount St. Mary's in Emmitsburg] . . . .Apart from the benefit to the Church, what immense advantages will the college not present in the way of Catholic education in a country where there is no alternative for the education of the young but to send them to England with its many temptations, or to place them in colleges where the lack of discipline is the smallest drawback.

The cornerstone was laid May 29, 1833, and less than four years later the seminary was destroyed by fire before the building was complete. There was no insurance, nor was there money to rebuild. Bishop John Hughes called the Nyack experience, "a splendid folly."

Lafargeville, Jefferson County (1838–40)

Bishop Dubois sent his Coadjutor Bishop, John Hughes, 300 miles north of New York, to investigate property John Lafarge was offering for a new seminary. There, at Lafargeville, on September 20th, 1838, St. Vincent de Paul Seminary was opened, to serve as both college and seminary. The great distance from New York was an advantage in the eyes of Bishop Dubois, who believed that the rural location would keep the students far away from "the temptation

and excitement of the great city." Yet Bishop Hughes would later concede, "the location . . . was found to be too remote from the city, and the seminarians with the teachers were transferred, in the autumn of 1841, to St. John's College at Fordham."

Top: Reverend Joseph O'Hare, S.J., Ph.D., and the Very Reverend Gerald L. Brown, S.S., Ph.D., during the Academic Procession.

Left: St. John's Hall, Fordham, N.Y., home of St. Joseph's Seminary from 1840-1861.

St. Joseph's Seminary, Fordham, Bronx (1840–61)

The failure of Lafargeville led Bishop Hughes to the purchase of Rose Hill Manor, at Fordham, in the Bronx.

Rose Hill was bought for about $30,000. To fit the buildings for the reception of students would cost, it was supposed, $10,000 more. To meet these demands the Bishop had, of course, not a penny; but he concluded the bargain, and immediately opened subscriptions through-

Whilst all this has been going on, I have plunged into a new and serious enterprise for the promotion of religion in this ecclesiastical province of New York.

That "serious enterprise" was the purchase of a Methodist University in the city of Troy to be used as the new Provincial Seminary of the Metropolitan See of New York. Initially, Hughes hoped to put it under the care of the Sulpicians of Paris, but the Sulpicians declined the invitation for fear that it might undermine their ability to staff their other seminaries in Baltimore and Montreal. Nevertheless, the seminary at Troy was opened in October, 1864. The death of Archbishop Hughes January 3, 1864, left the task of dedicating the new seminary on December 1, 1864, to his successor Archbishop John McCloskey.

Characteristics of the legendary "Trojan" spirit can be gleaned from the address made by the Most Reverend Patrick J. Hayes at the funeral of Troy's second president, Bishop Henry Gabriels:

"Discere et docere in Christo"—learn and teach in Christ, was the spirit that characterized Dr. Gabriels as president of St. Joseph's Seminary in Troy. . . . About 700 priests have come out of Troy bearing on their priestly minds and hearts the impress of the safe, sound and solid piety, scholarship and discipline they obtained under this just and saintly master in Israel, our beloved Dr. Gabriels.

out the diocese. A large part of the money was obtained in this way. A considerable sum was collected in Europe, and the balance was finally raised by loans in small amounts, for which interest was paid at the rate of five per cent.

From 1840 to 1846 the seminary was under the care of the Vincentian Fathers. From 1846 to 1856 the Jesuits directed the work of the seminary. Following the 1856 sale of the college property to the Jesuits, diocesan priests replaced the Jesuit faculty until 1861, when difficulty in maintaining a faculty of secular clergy, as well as the outbreak of the Civil War, caused Bishop Hughes to close the seminary at Fordham. In its twenty years of existence it ordained 107 priests.

> *Here is the school of Christ—*
> *the upper room—*
> *Where men shall learn to know*
> *the bud and bloom*
> *Of saintly lives; where Christ*
> *Himself shall teach . . . .*
> WM. LIVINGSTON, POET

Archbishop Michael A. Corrigan, successor to Cardinal McCloskey, desired to bring his seminary closer to the New York See, and so closed Troy in 1896, and sent more than 80 seminarians to the new seminary on Valentine Hill—DUNWOODIE.

—Italicized paragraphs from Reverend Arthur J. Scanlon, *St. Joseph's Seminary, Dunwoodie, N.Y., 1896–1921*

Saint Joseph's Provincial Seminary
Troy, New York (1864–96)

In the midst of the Civil War, Archbishop Hughes would write in 1862,

We were here for the first 10 years of Dunwoodie's life from 1896 to 1906. These were heady years. The Sulpicians at that time helped to put together what Christopher Kaufman called the foremost faculty of biblical scholars in Catholic higher education in

A comparison of the founding faculty of St. Joseph's Seminary and the faculty at the time of the seminary centennial reveals a marked similarity which is itself an expression of what Dunwoodie is. A combination of religious and diocesan priests formed the first faculty under Fr. Edward Dyer, S.S., D.D., a priest of the Society of St. Sulpice, known for both his firm grounding in the Sulpician tradition of priestly formation and keen awareness of the unique pastoral concerns and needs of the then-expanding Church in the United States. The centennial faculty, guided by Bishop Edwin F. O'Brien, S.T.D., is comprised of a combination of religious and diocesan priests, along with religious and lay men and women. Like the founding faculty, the centennial faculty combines a deep respect for and knowledge of the Tradition of the Church with an awareness of the need to guide the students as they seek to apply the lessons of this Tradition to the needs of the contemporary Church. The Tradition thus continues to enrich the Church as it is handed on faithfully to successive generations of Dunwoodie men.

Father Dyer sought to form the whole man into an effective priest. To that end, he insisted that the professors not be mere lecturers but real teachers whose expertise in their particular field would both be communicated to the students and incite in them a real desire for lifelong learning. He also urged both faculty and students alike to come to know each other and to that end encouraged faculty participation in student meals and activities. While not sacrificing the spiritual richness of the Sulpician tradition of seminary education, Fr. Dyer saw the need to educate the seminarians in the sciences, both physical and social, so that they might minister effectively in the modern world. This insistence that the priest be a man conversant in both the matters of the day and the timeless teaching of the Church remains as the foundational principle of the Dunwoodie education.

Similarly, faculty involvement in the day-to-day life of the seminarians remains a foundational prin-

the United States. . . . In 1903 Archbishop Farley asked the faculty to help publish "The New York Review" and for three years this prestigious journal gathered into one place the best thinking of the times. Joseph M. White called this period "the highpoint of intellectual vitality among the American clergy". . . . As we prepare for the new millennium . . . we respond to the challenge of John Paul II that we prepare holy priests capable of addressing the transcendent questions of our times and who will help build a civilization of love, in times very much like those of the shift from the 1890s into the 20th century.

THE VERY REVEREND
GERALD L. BROWN, S.S., PH.D.
PROVINCIAL OF THE SOCIETY OF ST. SULPICE
*WHICH PROVIDED FACULTY AND DIRECTED
THE ADMINISTRATION OF DUNWOODIE
IN ITS FIRST TEN YEARS.*

Left: The Dunwoodie Faculty, 1910
Right: The Dunwoodie Faculty, Centennial Year 1996-1997

ciple of the community life of the seminary.

The academic qualification of the Dunwoodie faculty has always been of the highest standard and represents the true catholicity of the Church. From its inception, the faculty has included those who have studied at a variety of universities throughout the world, with ecclesiastical degrees for those who teach the ecclesiastical sciences. The professors of the social sciences, along with those engaged in education in the arts, are alumni of some of the finest schools in their respective fields.

The academic expertise of St. Joseph's Seminary is linked with pastoral expertise. Since the early days, the faculty of the seminary has served the diocese in a variety of ways. The obvious academic enrichment of the clergy and laity easily comes to mind, but a very important facet of faculty life is the often overlooked service which the faculty provides in parishes throughout the Archdiocese of New York. Each Sunday, the majority of priest faculty members go to parishes as Sunday associates. In addition, members of the faculty are engaged in retreats and talks for parishes and particular groups. The Dunwoodie tradition of musical richness and excellence continues in the Festival Choir, which, under the direction of a faculty member, combines the seminary choir with singers from parishes throughout the Archdiocese. Seminary faculty also serve on the Metropolitan Tribunal, providing their expertise in the judgment of marriage cases and other canonical questions. All this expresses the fact that the Dunwoodie faculty are not just professors but are also priests, religious, and lay people willing to give of their talents for the good of the Church.

As Dunwoodie begins its second century, it looks forward to the continued enrichment of its faculty by new members blending with those whose expertise and insights bridge the generations of Dunwoodie students.

—E.W.

41

I want to acknowledge in a very special way a group of people who have given this seminary a very, very special life; a very, very special

CHANGING ROLES— FROM NURTURERS TO TEACHERS

As soon as a visitor enters the main hall of St. Joseph's Seminary, he will be greeted by four larger-than-life statues of American saints. Among these are St. Rose of Lima and St. Kateri Tekakwitha—their presence, a silent reminder of the sacrifices made by Catholic women for the Church. During the past 100 years, they have watched over the formation of generations of priests. They have not been the only women to do so.

When St. Joseph's Seminary opened its doors in 1896, the day-to-day domestic concerns of the seminary community were entrusted to the Sisters of Charity. The supervision of the kitchen, laundry, and housekeeping remained under their purview until 1934. One of the Sisters also served as infirmarian. In 1934, these duties were handed over to the Sisters of St. Joan of Bergerville, Quebec, who fulfilled them until the Spring of 1943. At that time, the Carmelite Sisters for the Aged and Infirm agreed to come to Dunwoodie. Although the extent of their duties changed over the years, the Carmelite Sisters remained in charge of many of the domestic areas of seminary life until 1972.

The 1965–66 academic year saw the entry of women into the academic sphere of the seminary's life. In that year, Dr. Elizabeth Salmon, a member of the Fordham University Philosophy Department, began a four-year tenure as Professor of Philosophy. Since then, a number of women, both lay and religious, have served on the Dunwoodie faculty in the fields of philosophy, theology, Scripture, church music, liturgy, catechetics, modern languages, speech and psychology. In addition, women have served on the faculty of both the Diaconate Formation Program and the Institute of Religious Studies. The current Dean of the Institute is a lay woman. Another aspect of the aca-

touch that could be said, of course, of many, but I refer most particularly to those women faculty members and staff members . . . who have given a new dimension, enriched and deepened our understanding beyond measure. . . . For example, the first woman ever to teach in the famed Institute for Biblical Studies, the Biblicum in Rome, was Sister Mary Timothea Elliott. She got her doctorate from the Biblicum and became accomplished in ten languages, and left the Biblicum to come teach here at St. Joseph's Seminary, Dunwoodie. This is the calibre of woman who has joined us.

JOHN CARDINAL O'CONNOR
ADDRESS AT ACADEMIC CONVOCATION

demic life of the seminary is, of course, the library. Since 1983 women have been working as professional librarians in the Archbishop Corrigan Memorial Library, and since 1985, the Director of the Library has been a woman religious.

Finally, over the years, women have contributed financially to the seminary, in small anonymous donations through their parishes, as well as in large gifts. The Cardinal Spellman Recreation Center was made possible by the very generous gift of Mrs. Mary McGovern in 1941.

Cooking and cleaning, teaching and guiding, helping to pay the bills—the women of Dunwoodie have, over the first century, contributed to the life of the seminary in the same way they contribute to the life of our society.   —M.E.H.

Opposite page, left to right: Statue of St. Rose of Lima, main hall, St. Joseph's Seminary; Cardinal John O'Connor approaching the speaker's platform during the Academic Procession.

This page, top to bottom: Mary Ellen Hubbard, Ph.D., Dean of the Institute of Religious Studies; Sister Mary Timothea Elliott, R.S.M., S.S.D., Professor of Scripture; Sister Maria Regina Melican, O.P., M.L.S., Librarian.

We, the seminarians of St. Joseph's Seminary, from the Archdioceses of New York, Rangoon, Duris,

1900: THE SEMINARIAN'S LIFE AT DUNWOODIE

by Reverend Francis P. Duffy, D.D., Canadian-born chaplain to the Sixty-Ninth New York Regiment during World War I. Father Duffy, recipient of the Distinguished Service Cross and Medal, the Croix de Guerre, and the Legion of Honor, spent 14 years at Dunwoodie teaching philosophy and theology. His statue, a tribute to his service during World War I, stands in Times Square.

The first twenty-four hours a student spends in seminary are devoted to putting in order the room which has been assigned him, arranging about his class, finding out the order of exercises, meeting old friends and making new ones. At the end of that time he finds himself suddenly launched into a week's retreat, during which silence and meditation, spiritual reading, the recitation of the office, and conferences from the professors all tend to give him a proper idea of the seriousness of life and the importance of the step he has taken. . . . Week follows week, unbroken except by the Wednesday holiday and Sunday and Holyday services.

At 5:30 every morning, winter and summer, the persistent bells jangle out their call to a new day's work. Immediately afterwards one of the students on each corridor knocks at the doors of his comrades and wakes them with a reminder of what the day's work ought to be, crying *Benedicamus Domino*, to which comes the response, *Deo Gratias*. And then *Laudetur Jesus Christus, In Aeternum*. . . . At 6 o'clock all repair to the meditation halls, and a half hour is spent in the saying of morning prayers and the making of meditation. Then all attend the Holy Sacrifice of the Mass in the beautiful chapel of the seminary, and those who receive Holy Communion remain for a thanksgiving Mass. . . . Breakfast is at 7:30, two hours after rising, and after breakfast the solemn silence which had prevailed since 8:30 the preceding evening is broken by recreation. At 8:15 all retire to their rooms to prepare for class, which is from 9 o'clock until 10. Then follows an hour of study, an hour of class and fifteen minutes of free time. . . . Dinner follows at 12:30, then the *Angelus* in the chapel and recreation until 2:30. There is a half hour's study at 2:30, and then class for an hour. Then . . . comes the "Long Study," from 4:15 until 6:15. The beads are recited in private, and supper follows at 6:30. Then the *Angelus* in the chapel, recreation until 7:45, study or class until 8:30, and

Tirana, and the dioceses of Lincoln, Sioux City, Beijing, Shanghai, the Franciscan Friars of the Renewal, and the Society of Mary, are proud and honored to participate in this celebration of Dunwoodie's Centennial. The academic and pastoral formation we are offered is truly extraordinary and for this we are deeply thankful. We are looking forward to being priests in our respective diocese and religious communities and pray for Dunwoodie's continued success as it forms priests for the next millennium.

DEACON MICHAEL MARTINE
CLASS OF 1997
*GREETINGS ON BEHALF OF THE
SEMINARIANS OF DUNWOODIE*

spiritual reading in common for half an hour. At 9 o'clock all meet once more in the chapel for night prayers. After prayers the sweet familiar hymn, *Adoro te devote*, is sung, and then, after some time in private devotions to the Blessed Sacrament, each student passes silently to his room, there to read his Bible or make a short spiritual reading, prepare the points of meditation for the following morning, and prepare for his night's rest. At 10 o'clock the lights are extinguished throughout the house.

Why are you here as seminarians? Why are you here, members of the faculty and others who prepare seminarians for the priesthood? Is it not to "know the mind of the Lord"? The seminarian must ask himself: Is Christ calling me? Does He wish me to be His priest? If you answer "yes," then the great work of the seminary is to help you to put off "the natural man," to leave behind "the old man," that is, the unspiritual man who used to be, in order to experience the action of the Holy Spirit and to understand the things of the spirit of God.

POPE JOHN PAUL II
ADDRESS AT DUNWOODIE

Opposite page, left to right: Class of 1900; Michael Martine, Class of 1997, House Deacon, representing St. Joseph's Seminary students, processing with Delisle Callender at front, representing Institute of Religious Studies students and Anne Marie Wadsley, M.A., at rear, representing I.R.S. Alumni Association.

This page, left to right: Seminarians at Statue of St. Patrick on Dunwoodie grounds, 1947. A 1997 group of seminarians reflects the diversity among the men now attending Dunwoodie.

I bring you the greetings and congratulations of the Pontifical University of St. Thomas Aquinas in Rome, which we all fondly know as the Angelicum. On this 100th Anniversary

PASTORES DABO VOBIS

The whole formation imparted to candidates for the priesthood aims at preparing them to enter into communion with the charity of Christ the good shepherd. Hence, their formation in its different aspects must have a fundamentally pastoral character. The Council's Decree, Optatam Totius, *states so clearly when speaking of major seminaries: "The whole training of the students should have as its object to make them true shepherds of souls after the example of our*

Lord Jesus Christ, teacher, priest, and shepherd. Hence, they should be trained for the ministry of the word so that they may gain an ever-increasing understanding of the revealed word of God, making it their own by meditation, and giving it expression in their speech and in their lives. They should be trained for the ministry of worship and sanctification, so that by prayer and the celebration of the sacred liturgical functions they may carry on in the work of salvation through the eucharistic sacrifice and the sacraments. They should be trained to undertake the ministry of the shepherd, that they may know how to represent Christ to humanity, Christ who 'did not come to have service done to him but to serve others and to give his life as a ransom for the lives of many . . .,' and that they may win over many by becoming the servants of all."

—Pope John Paul II, *Pastores Dabo Vobis*

Above: The Reverend John P. McGuire, O.P., S.T.D., Vice Rector, Pontifical University of St. Thomas Aquinas, Rome, addresses the convocation.

of St. Joseph's Seminary, we are proud to acknowledge our relationship with your venerable center of priestly formation.

We mutually endeavor to instill in our students a love of learning which will find its fullest expression in a love of God's people. Your graduates over a 100-year period have fashioned the Catholic life of the great Archdiocese of New York whose vitality is ensured by the wonderful young men it continues to send forth from this esteemed institution. We are proud of our association with St. Joseph's Seminary, many of whose graduates continue their higher education at our university in Rome.

THE VERY REVEREND JOHN P. MCGUIRE, O.P., S.T.D., VICE RECTOR, PONTIFICAL UNIVERSITY OF ST. THOMAS AQUINAS, ROME

Saint Joseph's Seminary exists primarily for the formation of candidates for the priesthood of the Catholic Church. Its responsibility, therefore, encompasses the human, spiritual, intellectual, pastoral and cultural formation of its students.

The Spiritual Year consists of a specialized program which concentrates on human and spiritual formation. This is followed by the academic course which comprises eight semesters of professional study with concentration on theology and allied disciplines. After six semesters a student is eligible for the degree of Master of Divinity. Upon completion of this degree qualified students may apply for the Master of Arts in Theology available during the fourth year of study.

At the end of six semesters of professional study, the seminarians are evaluated by the Rector and

Corners: Four stained glass windows from the sacristy of the SS. Peter and Paul Chapel, depict the stages of ordination prior to the revisions of the Second Vatican Council.

faculty for presentation as worthy candidates for ordination to the Order of Deacon. Ordination to the Order of Priest follows the conclusion of the fourth year.

While the prescribed courses offer an intensive preparation for pastoral ministry on the parish level, special priestly assignments in areas such as education, social work, military chaplaincy, and diocesan administration require further graduate studies which are usually undertaken after ordination in preparation for such positions.

Human Formation

It is important that the priest should mold his human personality in such a way that it becomes a bridge and not an obstacle for others in their meeting with Jesus Christ the Redeemer of humanity. Future priests should therefore cultivate a series of human qualities, not only out of proper and due growth and realization of self, but also with a view to the ministry. . . . A simple and demanding program for this human formation can be found in the words of the apostle Paul to the Philippians: "Whatever is true, whatever is honorable, whatever is just, whatever is pure, whatever is lovely, whatever is gracious, if there is any excellence, if there is anything worthy of praise, think about these things" (Phil 4:8).

—Pope John Paul II
Pastores Dabo Vobis

initiate into it the flock committed to them. They should be taught to seek Christ in the faithful meditation on God's word, in the active participation in the sacred mysteries of the Church, especially in the Eucharist and in the divine office, in the bishop

Spiritual Formation

The spiritual training . . . should be imparted in such a way that the students might learn to live in an intimate and unceasing union with the Father through His Son Jesus Christ in the Holy Spirit. Conformed to Christ the Priest through their sacred ordination they should be accustomed to adhere to Him as friends, in an intimate companionship, their whole life through. They should so live His paschal mystery themselves that they can

who sends them and in the people to whom they are sent, especially the poor, the children, the sick, the sinners and the unbelievers.

—Vatican Council II, *Optatam Totius*

Intellectual Formation

The intellectual formation of candidates for the priesthood finds its specific justification in the very nature of the ordained ministry, and the challenge of the "new evangelization" to

TO BE WITH CHRIST

He then went up the mountain and summoned the men he himself had decided on, who came and joined him. He named twelve as his companions whom he would send to preach the good news.

MARK 3:13-14

which our Lord is calling the Church on the threshold of the third millennium shows just how important this formation is. . . . The present situation is heavily marked by religious indifference, by a widespread mistrust regarding the real

Pastoral Formation

Pastoral study and action direct one to an inner source, which the work of formation will take care to guard and made good use of: This is the ever-deeper communion with the pastoral charity of Jesus, which—just as it was the principle and driving force of his salvific action—likewise, thanks to the outpouring of the Holy Spirit in the sacrament of orders, should constitute the principle and driving force of the priestly ministry. It is a question of a type of formation meant not only to ensure scientific, pastoral competence and practical skill, but also and especially a way of being in communion with the very sentiments and behavior of Christ the good shepherd: "Have this mind among yourselves, which is yours in Christ Jesus" (Phil 2:5).

—Pope John Paul II
Pastores Dabo Vobis

capacity of reason to reach objective and universal truth, and by fresh problems and questions brought up by scientific and technological discoveries. It strongly demands a high level of intellectual formation, such as will enable priests to proclaim, in a context like this, the changeless Gospel of Christ and to make it credible to the legitimate demands of human reason.

—Pope John Paul II
Pastores Dabo Vobis

Opposite page, left to right: Celebrating with friends and family on Family Festival Day; Adoration of the Blessed Sacrament at the chapel of Mary Immaculate Seminary, Northampton, site of Sprituality Year.

This page, left to right: On-Line at the Archbishop Corrigan Library; Seminary tour, Family Festival Day.

Curiosity brought Larry O'Toole to the Diaconate Formation Program at Dunwoodie. He was attending Mass one Sunday when he noticed a man in the sanctuary wearing vestments he was not familiar with. Larry is now very familiar with the stole and dalmatic of the Office of Deacon. It has been his privilege to wear them since his ordination to the permanent diaconate one year ago.

Deacon O'Toole was sponsored by the pastor of St. Augustine's Parish, New City, N.Y., the community in which he lives and serves out his canonical assignment. Following ordination Deacon O'Toole's employer made him an offer which he gratefully accepted when he took off his hat as Director of Safety and Security for the New York Medical College to become the college's first full-time university chaplain. His ministry to the students revolves

around the desire of the students and administration to create a Catholic identity for the Medical College in a unique community where science and spirituality must complement each other.

Judy O'Toole supported her husband of 33 years during the formation process. Because of their years of active involvement in the Church, Judy saw the diaconate as a natural progression for Larry. Judy laughs: "Here we are, launching our children, and we finally have some free space and time. I really had to think about whether or not the diaconate was what I wanted to fill that time." The partnership between Larry and Judy is not uncommon among the married deacons. As couples, they are a witness to the Sacrament of Matrimony. Participation in the diaconate has only expanded and enriched their witness to the presence of Christ among us.

25 YEARS OF DIACONATE FORMATION— "PRAYER, SERVICE, SACRAMENT"

During its centennial year, Dunwoodie hosted the 25th anniversary celebration of the Permanent Diaconate Formation Program of the Archdiocese of New York. During the Mass to celebrate this Jubilee, Cardinal O'Connor quoted from documents of the early Church Fathers which describe the office of the deacon as nothing other than "the ministry of Jesus Christ. . . . The deacons too, who are ministers of the mysteries of Jesus Christ, should please all in every way; for they are not servants of food and drink, but ministers of the Church of God. . . . They represent Jesus Christ, just as the bishop has the role of Father, and the presbyters are like God's council and an apostolic band. You cannot have a church without these." The Cardinal underscored this last statement by saying, "Those are strong words."

It was the Second Vatican Council which decided to restore the diaconate for the Western Church. The Council briefly described the nature and functions of the diaconate in the *Dogmatic Constitution of the Church, Lumen Gentium.* Pope Paul VI, implementing the

E FORMATION

Council's decisions, published new norms for the diaconate in his 1972 Apostolic Letter, *Ad Pascendum.*

The Diaconate Formation Program was introduced into the Archdiocese of New York by Terence Cardinal Cooke. The current four-year program, conducted in both English and Spanish, is designed to immerse a candidate in an integrated curriculum of spiritual, theological, and pastoral formation.

The three general areas of diaconal ministry are Charity, Word, and Liturgy. In the Archdiocese of New York, the Ministry of Charity is exercised through work with the sick, the elderly, the bereaved, and those who are in nursing homes. Some assist the St. Vincent de Paul Society, as well as apostolic activities of the laity. Proclaiming the Gospel at liturgy, preaching at baptisms, marriages, and wakes, and preparing people for the Sacraments of Initiation and Matrimony are some of the ways in which deacons serve in the Ministry of the Word. Assisting the bishop and the priest during liturgical celebrations, administering Baptism, distributing Holy Eucharist, and bringing Viaticum to the dying, are among the ways in which the deacon serves in the Ministry of the Liturgy. —D.M.

Above, top to bottom: Mass celebrating the 25th anniversary of the Permanent Diaconate Program in the main seminary chapel—Processional; Cardinal O'Connor offering the opening prayer; some of the deacon's wives.

Facing page: Deacon Lawrence O'Toole with his wife Judy, in the seminary cloister; Monsignor Thomas J. Bergin, M.A., Vicar for Education, Archdiocese of New York.

LAY EDUCATION AT ST. JOSEPH'S SEMINARY

In 1971, the Sacred Congregation for the Clergy published *The General Cathechetical Directory* which called for the establishment of "higher institutes of catechetics" to assure that the catechetical and religious education work of the Church would be in the hands of well-trained people. The Congregation called for these institutes to "set university standards with regard to the curriculum, length of courses and conditions for admission."

Terence Cardinal Cooke took seriously this call. In 1975, he asked the Secretary for Education, Monsignor Joseph O'Keefe, and two of his associates, Father Dennis Fernandes and Father Michael Wrenn, to investigate the possibility of establishing just such an institute in the Archdiocese. As a result of their work, the Archdiocesan Catechetical Institute, now the Institute of Religious Studies, opened its doors in the Spring of 1976 at St. Joseph's Seminary, under the direction of Father Wrenn. The Institute offered a fully accredited Master's degree comprising 30 credits of course

When St. Joseph's Seminary was 80 years old it received a new mission from Terence Cardinal Cooke, then Archbishop of New York. In addition to forming men for the priesthood, the Cardinal charged the seminary with the task of forming catechetical leaders for the

work and a written comprehensive examination. Since 1983, the degree has been a Master of Arts in Religious Studies.

The program provided by the Institute proved to be of great use to the people of the Archdiocese. In the Fall of 1978, an off-campus site was opened at the Redemptorist Seminary in Esopus (Ulster County) to serve people in the upstate counties. The Institute soon outgrew its original home. In 1983, the administrative offices and classrooms moved out of the main seminary building into the old convent. In 1988, the Esopus site

Kelly Anderson, graduate of the Institute of Religious Studies, 1996, has another connection to Dunwoodie. Her great-grandfather, William Schickel, was the architect hired by Archbishop Corrigan to build St. Joseph's Seminary.

voice which
ty, and ou
Church to
nary for pr
as well as a
quality and
Institute, a
students at
necessary t
priests and
the seminai
that reflects
centuries to

GREE
OF TI

Archdiocese. The Archdiocesan Catechetical Institute was founded to fulfill that mission by providing a graduate-level program leading to a Master's Degree. Over the years as the structures for preparing catechists in the Archdiocese have changed and as more and more lay people have come to St. Joseph's looking for systematic teaching of Catholic doctrine which is faithful to the magisterium, the scope of the Institute's work has expanded. The St. Joseph's Seminary Institute of Religious Studies, as it is now known, is the means by which the seminary provides education for those involved in the work of the Church and those who desire to know and live their faith more fully, especially among the laity.

MARY ELLEN HUBBARD, PH.D., DEAN,
INSTITUTE OF RELIGIOUS STUDIES

1993, in 1988 and 1989.

As of June 7, 1997, the Institute had awarded 371 Master's degrees, 76% of them to lay people. Most live and work in the Archdiocese of New York and other dioceses in the New York area. Many of the Institute's graduates are actively engaged in the educational mission of the Church, in the Catholic elementary and secondary schools, in parish religious education programs, serving on parish liturgy committees, coordinating and teaching in RCIA programs, running youth ministry programs, directing retreats, and working in public advocacy.

There are still some priests, deacons and religious studying at the Institute, but most of the students are now lay people. This preparation of lay people through a rigorous and thorough Master of Arts program, faithful to the magisterium, rounds out the comprehensive means by which the seminary is helping the Church in New York to prepare for the third millennium. As John Paul II has said, "Only within the Church, the mother and teacher of man, is it possible to outline a model of the priest and lay person we would like to form on the threshold of the third millennium." Dunwoodie, as the major seminary of the Archdiocese, provides the ecclesial context *par excellence* for educating and forming the laity to fulfill their rightful roles in the mission of the Church.

—M.E.H.

stude
life ai

T
from
tion (
few p
an ai
inter
to co
opera
throu
the d
sive
and (

A
logic
to re
Cath
wher
form
dates

was moved to Our Lady of Hope Center in Balmville, also in Ulster County. This site was moved again in the Fall of 1996 to Poughkeepsie in Dutchess County. At the request of Cardinal O'Connor, who wanted the Institute's program to be available to even more people in the Archdiocese, two new off-campus sites in Staten Island and Manhattan were opened by Father Ferdinando Berardi, Dean of the Institute from 1987 to

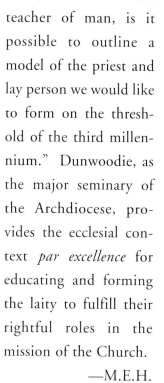

Since the laity . . . live in the midst of the world and its concerns, they are called by God to exercise their Apostolate in the world like leaven, with the ardor of the Spirit of Christ.
VATICAN II, *APOSTOLICAM ACTUOSITATEM*

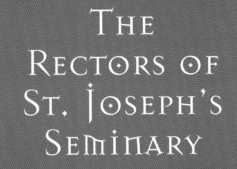

THE RECTORS OF ST. JOSEPH'S SEMINARY

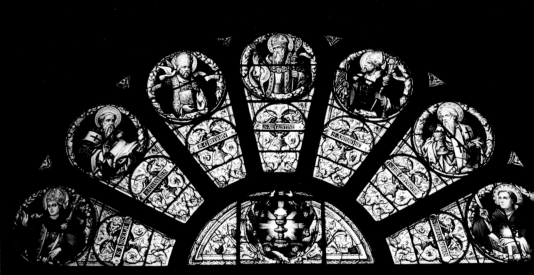

Th

ap
do
bu
or
m
to
a
p.
m
st
L
L
b
b
d
i
b

T

b
J
$

1896-1902   Edward R. Dyer, S.S., D.D.

Dunwoodie's first rector was originally from Washington, D.C. He joined the Society of St. Sulpice in France and was ordained in 1879. He earned his doctorate in theology in 1884.

1902-1909   James F. Driscoll, S.S., D.D.

The second rector was a fellow Sulpician and close personal friend of Father Dyer. He was an accomplished Scripture scholar. During his administration, Dunwoodie enjoyed a high academic reputation.

1909-1922   John P. Chidwick, D.D.

Monsignor Chidwick, an alumnus of Manhattan College, was ordained at St. Joseph's Seminary in Troy. His heroic service aboard the U.S.S. Maine during the Spanish-American War made him a popular figure in New York, so much so, that he was invited to address the New York State Assembly on February 8, 1899.

1922-1930   James T. McEntyre, D.D.

The fourth rector of the seminary was a graduate of the Grand Séminaire in Montreal. He edified his seminarians by his devotion to the Blessed Sacrament and to the cancer patients at Rosary Hill in Hawthorne, New York.

1931-1940   Arthur J. Scanlan, D.D.

Monsignor Scanlan was ordained from Dunwoodie in 1907 and was the first alumnus to become rector of the seminary. In 1940, he became the first pastor of St. Helena's parish in the Bronx.

1940-1956   John M. A. Fearns, S.T.D.

The sixth rector of the seminary was ordained from the North American College in Rome in 1922. He was only forty-three years old when he was appointed rector. In December 1957, he was named an Auxiliary Bishop of New York.

1956-1958   Charles O'C. Sloane, L.L.B., S.S.L., S.T.L.

Although Monsignor Charles O'Conor Sloane was rector for only two years, he taught Scripture at the seminary for seventeen years. In 1958, he was appointed pastor of Saint Peter and Saint Paul's in Mount Vernon, N.Y.

1958-1962   Francis F. Reh, S.T.L., J.C.D.

After serving as vice-rector of the North American College in Rome, Monsignor Reh was appointed the rector of Dunwoodie. During his administration the seminary received Middle States Accreditation. He was named Bishop of Saginaw in 1969.

1962-1964   Thomas A. Donnellan, J.C.D.

Monsignor Donnellan served as rector of the seminary during the Second Vatican Council. He was appointed Bishop of Ogdensburg in 1964, and on July 16, 1968, he was named Archbishop of Atlanta. He served there until his death in 1987.

Top: Doctors of the Church, stained glass window from the Chapel of SS. Peter and Paul, Dunwoodie.

1964-1968   Edwin B. Broderick, Ph.D.

Monsignor Broderick served as rector during the turbulent years of the Vietnam War, the civil rights movement and student unrest on college campuses. He was named an Auxiliary Bishop in 1967 and appointed Bishop of Albany in 1969.

1968-1973   Edward J. Montano, S.T.D.

Monsignor Montano taught philosophy at the seminary for 18 years and was named rector in 1968. After serving in that office for five years, he was appointed pastor of Sacred Heart Parish in Suffern. He returned to the seminary in 1982 to teach theology.

1973-1979   Austin B. Vaughan, S.T.D., D.D.

The seminary's twelfth rector was ordained in 1951 from the North American College in Rome. In 1977, he was made an Auxiliary Bishop, and the following year appointed pastor of St. Patrick's Church in Newburgh, N.Y.

1979-1982   John J. Mescall, M.S.

Monsignor Mescall, a priest with broad pastoral experience, was appointed rector by Cardinal Cooke in 1979. He had been the spiritual director of the seminary and served the Archdiocese as the Vicar for Religious before coming to Dunwoodie.

1982-1985   Edward M. Connors, Ph.D.

Monsignor Connors came to the seminary with a strong academic background. He had served as the Superintendent of Schools and as the Secretary of Education. In 1985, he returned to his beloved parish, Immaculate Heart of Mary, in Scarsdale, N.Y., as pastor.

1985-1989   Edwin F. O'Brien, S.T.D.

Cardinal O'Connor appointed his secretary, Monsignor O'Brien as the new rector of the seminary in 1985. Prior to this, Monsignor O'Brien had served as a parish priest, army chaplain, Director of Communications for the Archdiocese and secretary to Cardinal Cooke and Cardinal O'Connor.He left Dunwoodie in 1989 to serve as rector of the North American College, Rome.

1990-1993   Raymond T. Powers, S.T.D.

Monsignor Powers was a former faculty member of the seminary and had served as the vice-rector of the North American College in Rome. He had served at the Apostolic Delegation in Washington, and was a pastor of St. Paul's Church in Congers, N.Y.

1994-1997   Edwin F. O'Brien, S.T.D.

In 1994, Cardinal O'Connor once again appointed Monsignor O'Brien the rector of the seminary. When he was named Auxiliary Bishop of N.Y., Bishop O'Brien chose for his motto the Latin phrase: *Pastores Dabo Vobis*, the title of an Apostolic Exhortation by Pope John Paul II which deals with the formation of priests. In 1997 he was named Coadjutor Archbishop of the Archdiocese for Military Services, U.S.A.

1997-   Francis J. McAree, S.T.D.

Monsignor McAree has served as a professor of systematic theology at Dunwoodie since 1981. From 1993-1994 he was acting rector, and from 1994-1997 he was vice-rector. He earned a licentiate and a doctorate in sacred theology at the Gregorian University, Rome.

—R.M.

Christ gives the dignity of a royal priesthood to the people he has made his own. From these, with a brother's love, he chooses men to share his sacred ministry by the laying on of hands. He calls them to lead your holy people in love, nourish them by your word and strengthen them through the sacraments. Father, they are to give their lives in your service and for the salvation of your people as they grow in the likeness of Christ and honor you by their courageous witness of faith and love.

—FROM THE PREFACE
OF THE CHRISM MASS,
THE SACRAMENTARY

St. Joseph's Seminary Continuing the Work of Salvation

Centennial Alumni Day October 15, 1996

I f you gather a group of Dunwoodie Alumni together and ask them about their seminary years, one will no doubt say, with a smile and a twinkle in his eye, "The best view I ever had of Dunwoodie was in my rear-view mirror as I was driving away on my last day!" Like any other university student, he will then tell you his war stories and humorous anecdotes. But then he will also tell you about the men with whom he lived, studied, prayed and was ordained. As he speaks, you will hear one constant theme: *Fraternity.*

The respect, pride and affection that he expresses for his fellow classmates are things he shares with every alumnus, no matter what year he crossed the threshold of Dunwoodie. Today, as you walk through the main corridor of the seminary, you will see their pictures hanging there—the men of Dunwoodie. Listening to their stories, you will come to understand something about the spirit of brotherhood which animates their lives and assists them in carrying out their priestly calling.

"What got me through was the spirit of the other guys," is how a member of the

> *You have carried out this mission of Christ, our high priest, with exquisite beauty.*
> CARDINAL O'CONNOR
> *TO THE PRIESTS GATHERED AT THE ALUMNI DAY MASS*

Above: The Agony of Jesus in the Garden, detail from a stained glass window in the chapel of SS. Peter and Paul, Dunwoodie. The full window, seen on the previous page, is paired with the Old Testament image of Jacob Grieving for His Son, Joseph.

Left: Alumni Mass.

class of '72 speaks about St. Joseph's during the turbulent years of the '60s and '70s. "Those were tough times, 'the age of Aquarius.' But we were all clear about what we had to do and kept each other focused."

The seminarians on Valentine Hill may have studied apart from others, but they were not immune to the challenges of their own day. These may have taken the form of the Church's reaction to Modernism which took its toll on the academic life at Dunwoodie; or the cost-cutting efficiencies of Procurator John J. Donovan which kept the lights out, the heat low, and stomachs rumbling during the Depression. As one alumnus from the class of '39 puts it, "It made for great bonding among the men. There was never a class closer than the 39ers." There were the air-raid drills and victory gardens of the W.W.II era, during which 147 Dunwoodie alumni served as chaplains, three dying while in uniform.

In its 100th year, seminary enrollment is still recovering from the effects of the social and political upheaval of the '60s and early '70s. Msgr. Ferdinando Berardi, class of '77, tells a humorous anecdote of his first Holy Thursday as a seminarian: "I was the Master of Ceremonies. Some of the fellows had been sent down to the Cathedral. Of those remaining, there were twelve seminarians having their feet washed in the sanctuary, a little *schola* singing in the choir loft, and the servers. That left only four semi-

narians sitting out as the congregation! From that experience we decided to open up the services to the public the following year." The numbers may have been low, but Msgr. Berardi says, "we developed strong relationships with each other."

Fraternity. The Second Vatican Council's *Decree on the Ministry and Life of Priests* emphasizes this attribute of priestly life whereby each priest "is united in special bonds of Apostolic charity, ministry, and brotherhood with other members of this priesthood."

The men of Dunwoodie have many stories to tell, but they are united by fraternal bonds, forged during their seminary days, consecrated by the Sacrament of Holy Orders, and based in the single aspiration they all share—to be priests after the heart of Christ.   —D.M.

*N*ext year, St. Joseph's Seminary will celebrate its 100th anniversary. It is providential that the same year, 1996, will be a year of evangelization in the church in New York. It helps us remember the countless souls, redeemed by the blood of Christ, who have been helped toward salvation by the thousands of priests trained in this seminary. You will join them in continuing the work of salvation, which will never end until, as Jesus prayed, all will become one in him as he is one with the Father.
—POPE JOHN PAUL II
ADDRESS AT DUNWOODIE

Reverend Monsignor Ferdinando Berardi, '77, Administrator

Archdiocesan Director of the Society for the Propagation of the Faith

As Director of the Society for the Propagation of the Faith in New York, Monsignor Berardi

spends most of his time promoting mission awareness in parishes and schools. Considering the number of missionaries, religious orders and bishops from around the world who come to his office for assistance, one can easily forget that for most of the 19th century, Europe considered New York to be mission territory. In 1828 the Sacred Congregation for the Propagation of the Faith informed the Society in Lyons, that New York had the most pressing needs of any mission diocese in the world. Indeed, it was from the Society that Bishop Dubois and later Archbishop Hughes sought financial assistance in their respective efforts to build, furnish and maintain a seminary in the Archdiocese of New York. It is fitting, then, that a son of Dunwoodie should find himself intimately involved in the type of mission work that not too long ago helped provide the foundation of what has become one of the most influential archdioceses in the world.

While Msgr. Berardi's primary purpose is to procure assistance for the foreign missions, he actually spends a lot of time in New York parishes. His normal routine is to spend a weekend at a parish and preach on behalf of the Society at all of the masses. "It can be fun," he says. "I get to meet parishioners and see all of the work the Church is doing."

Msgr. Berardi says the response to the missions is tremendous. That may be due in part to his belief that he is not there simply to raise funds. He is also there to raise awareness of the world community and the heroic efforts that are undertaken by men and women of the Church to bring the Word of God to the entire world. Msgr. Berardi remembers that as a child, "what I was attracted to in the priesthood wasn't the diocesan priesthood. When you are young, you think big, romantic: I wanted to be a missionary. You must begin with idealism."

He says that today, "we are too focused on ourselves. Some people ask me why we should support the missions when we have so many needs at home. Yes, we do, and we always will have them. But Jesus said, 'Go and teach the whole world.' That is what the disciples were taught. Don't stay in Jerusalem. If we wait until we have everything in order, we'll never go anywhere. Mission work instills in us a greater sense of the universal Church."

Reverend Eric Raaser, '89, Educator

Teacher and Associate Dean of Students, Archbishop Stepinac High School, White Plains, N.Y.

"Whenever you talk spirituality in the classroom, it is a magic moment. You can hear a pin drop," says Father Eric Raaser, teacher and Associate Dean of Students at Archbishop Stepinac High School in White Plains, N.Y. He adds, "I think a lot of times we underestimate the spirituality of young people. They are looking for God, craving God." It is at times like this that Fr. Raaser knows the importance of having a priest in the classroom. It is not unusual for students class of '72 speaks about St. Joseph's during the turbulent years of the '60s and '70s. "Those were tough times, 'the age of Aquarius.' But we were all clear about what we had to do and kept each other focused."

The seminarians on Valentine Hill may have studied apart from others, but they were not immune to the challenges of their own day. These may have taken the form of the Church's reaction to Modernism which took its toll on the academic life at Dunwoodie; or the cost-cutting efficiencies of Procurator John J. Donovan which kept the lights out, the heat low, and stomachs rumbling during the Depression. As one alumnus from the class of '39 puts it, "It made for great bonding among the men. There was never a class closer than the 39ers." There were the air-raid drills and victory gardens of the W.W.II era, during which 147 Dunwoodie alumni served as chaplains, three dying while in uniform.

In its 100th year, seminary enrollment is still recovering from the effects of the social and political upheaval of the '60s and early '70s. Msgr. Ferdinando Berardi, class of '77, tells a humorous anecdote of his first Holy Thursday as a seminarian: "I was the Master of Ceremonies. Some of the fellows had been sent down to the Cathedral. Of those remaining, there were twelve seminarians having their feet washed in the sanctuary, a little *schola* singing in the choir loft, and the servers. That left only four semi-

Next year, St. Joseph's Seminary will celebrate its 100th anniversary. It is providential that the same year, 1996, will be a year of evangelization in the church in New York. It helps us remember the countless souls, redeemed by the blood of Christ, who have been helped toward salvation by the thousands of priests trained in this seminary. You will join them in continuing the work of salvation, which will never end until, as Jesus prayed, all will become one in him as he is one with the Father.

—POPE JOHN PAUL II
ADDRESS AT DUNWOODIE

narians sitting out as the congregation! From that experience we decided to open up the services to the public the following year." The numbers may have been low, but Msgr. Berardi says, "we developed strong relationships with each other."

Fraternity. The Second Vatican Council's *Decree on the Ministry and Life of Priests* emphasizes this attribute of priestly life whereby each priest "is united in special bonds of Apostolic charity, ministry, and brotherhood with other members of this priesthood."

The men of Dunwoodie have many stories to tell, but they are united by fraternal bonds, forged during their seminary days, consecrated by the Sacrament of Holy Orders, and based in the single aspiration they all share—to be priests after the heart of Christ.   —D.M.

> *Back to this retreat shall they come from time to time to renew the spirit of their exalted vocation, and to go forth, thus renewed, to continue their great work.*
> -ARCHBISHOP PATRICK J. RYAN, ADDRESS AT THE LAYING OF THE CORNERSTONE MAY 17, 1891

ALUMNI CELEBRATE THE CENTENNIAL OF THEIR ALMA MATER

Cardinal O'Connor praised the more than 300 priests concelebrating Mass with him in the SS. Peter and Paul Chapel at St. Joseph's Seminary in Dunwoodie for "being the priests this seminary trained you to be." The occasion was the annual Alumni Mass, which this year was part of the seminary's celebration of its 100th anniversary.

The Cardinal urged them to make this Mass "a mighty prayer that all priests of the Archdiocese of New York, past, present and future, will experience the joy one day of being priests united with Christ, our high priest." Principal concelebrants were Bishop Edwin B.

Broderick, Retired Bishop of Albany, and Bishops Patrick J. Sheridan, Vicar General; Edwin F. O'Brien, Rector; Anthony F. Mestice, and Austin B. Vaughan.

Cardinal O'Connor told the priests: "You have carried out this mission of Christ, our high priest, with exquisite beauty." These priests, according to the Cardinal, have sought "to give freedom to the captive, to bring truth to the uneducated, to feed the hungry, to house the homeless, to clothe the naked, to fight for justice for people of all races. This is what you have done. This is what you are; this is what you represent, and all of it is enshrined in this great Seminary of St. Joseph. I am proud, indeed, to be an honorary alumnus. I congratulate all of you for having made this seminary what it is, for contributing to the seminary as you do, but above all for being the priests this seminary trained you to be. It never fails, whether in the poorest parish or the most affluent one. This is the rule, not the exception. These people know our concerns for the poor, for the prisoners and for those in need, whatever their need might be."

Cardinal O'Connor was high in his praise for Dunwoodie. "This seminary has to bow its head to no seminary in the United States." He conceded there have been hard times, citing in particular the period after the Second Vatican Council when all seminaries faced difficult times because of the changes that were necessary. But Dunwoodie never completely folded, he added. "For every weakness," the Cardinal reminded the alumni, "there has been far more to talk about in strengths. For every little valley there has been far more of a prevailing peak." A factor in this regard has been Bishop O'Brien, who guided the planning of the events for the centennial year. Cardinal O'Connor said that Bishop O'Brien "is considered to be one of the greatest rectors in the United States."

At the end of Mass, the Cardinal cautioned the priests "not to let yourself get discouraged" over the shortage of vocations. He expects a change, noting the increased interest on the part of men of all ages in the evenings, weekends and retreats that he has held for those considering the priesthood. "A few years after the turn of the century," he said, "we're going to see a tremendous increase in vocations. I know that will be the case."

After Mass, the annual dinner was served at which Bishop Broderick was the speaker. A former Rector of Dunwoodie, he is a member of the class of 1942.

—G.J.H./*CNY*

*Facing page, counterclockwise, starting from upper right:
the seminary choir; communion; the class of 1990; procession; Msgr. Edward O'Donnell, '54, accepting the first Terence Cardinal Cooke Distinguished Alumnus Award for his service as the Director of Personnel for the Archdiocese; looking for old friends; youth and experience.*

Reverend Monsignor Ferdinando Berardi, '77, Administrator

Archdiocesan Director of the Society for the Propagation of the Faith

As Director of the Society for the Propagation of the Faith in New York, Monsignor Berardi

spends most of his time promoting mission awareness in parishes and schools. Considering the number of missionaries, religious orders and bishops from around the world who come to his office for assistance, one can easily forget that for most of the 19th century, Europe considered New York to be mission territory. In 1828 the Sacred Congregation for the Propagation of the Faith informed the Society in Lyons, that New York had the most pressing needs of any mission diocese in the world. Indeed, it was from the Society that Bishop Dubois and later Archbishop Hughes sought financial assistance in their respective efforts to build, furnish and maintain a seminary in the Archdiocese of New York. It is fitting, then, that a son of Dunwoodie should find himself intimately involved in the type of mission work that not too long ago helped provide the foundation of what has become one of the most influential archdioceses in the world.

While Msgr. Berardi's primary purpose is to procure assistance for the foreign missions, he actually spends a lot of time in New York parishes. His normal routine is to spend a weekend at a parish and preach on behalf of the Society at all of the masses. "It can be fun," he says. "I get to meet parishioners and see all of the work the Church is doing."

Msgr. Berardi says the response to the missions is tremendous. That may be due in part to his belief that he is not there simply to raise funds. He is also there to raise awareness of the world community and the heroic efforts that are undertaken by men and women of the Church to bring the Word of God to the entire world. Msgr. Berardi remembers that as a child, "what I was attracted to in the priesthood wasn't the diocesan priesthood. When you are young, you think big, romantic: I wanted to be a missionary. You must begin with idealism."

He says that today, "we are too focused on ourselves. Some people ask me why we should support the missions when we have so many needs at home. Yes, we do, and we always will have them. But Jesus said, 'Go and teach the whole world.' That is what the disciples were taught. Don't stay in Jerusalem. If we wait until we have everything in order, we'll never go anywhere. Mission work instills in us a greater sense of the universal Church."

Reverend Eric Raaser, '89, Educator

Teacher and Associate Dean of Students, Archbishop Stepinac High School, White Plains, N.Y.

"Whenever you talk spirituality in the classroom, it is a magic moment. You can hear a pin drop," says Father Eric Raaser, teacher and Associate Dean of Students at Archbishop Stepinac High School in White Plains, N.Y. He adds, "I think a lot of times we underestimate the spirituality of young people. They are looking for God, craving God." It is at times like this that Fr. Raaser knows the importance of having a priest in the classroom. It is not unusual for students to seek him out before or after class to ask, "Father, can I talk to you?" It is important for young people to have this type of access. "They have great respect for the priests," Fr. Raaser says of the students, "and Stepinac has given many priests to the Archdiocese. I think it is because of the role model of the priests who are here."

Father Raaser admits that the primary reason parents send their sons to Stepinac may have more to do with the safe and disciplined environment the school provides, than the fact that they are receiving a Catholic education. But this does not concern him. "Once you get them into the building and provide them with effective teachers and administrators, you can change hearts and help them discover the types of values that will enrich their spiritual lives. They are honest about the impact you have on them. I say, 'I don't care if you don't remember my name, but just remember that there was a priest who cared about you.'"

Father Raaser remembers the priest who cared about him. "I couldn't make up my mind about whether or not to pursue a vocation. The seed was planted by my mother, who sang in the church choir and at weddings when I was a child. I forgot about those things in high school. I was up in the air about the priesthood and then there was a priest in Newark who said, 'Look, try it out. Stop thinking about it. Live a life as close as possible to the priesthood, and see.'" He took the priest's advice. "I've been a priest for twelve years, and I can honestly say that I have never regretted it, never had a moment of doubt."

Reverend S. Keith Outlaw, '85, Parish Ministry
Administrator, St. Augustine's Parish, Bronx, N.Y.

At the age of 16, Keith Outlaw knew something about loss. By that time he had experienced the death of his mother, and a short year later, his father's death followed. His good friend Joe Taylor brought him home for visits. And then, one day, the Taylor family of six children and two parents invited him to stay. His friend Joe became his brother, and Mr. and Mrs. Taylor would, over a course of years, become "Mom" and "Dad." The Taylors gave the young Keith a home, a strong family life and a chance to learn about the Catholic Faith when he accompanied them to weekly Sunday Mass.

After graduating from Bowdoin College in 1979, he began instruction to enter the Church, and on December 20th, 1980, Keith was baptized and confirmed. His sponsor, Joe Taylor, the young man who brought Keith into his family, stood by his side as Keith was received into the greater family of the faithful.

While he was working at his career, a friend of the family, Monsignor Tim Collins, then pastor of SS. Philip and James Church in the Bronx, asked Keith to consider the possibility of a priestly vocation. While on retreat watching a film on the life of Christ, Keith was deeply moved by the scenes of Jesus' being nailed to the cross. What followed was a meditation on the consequences of injustice, the suffering of the innocent, and a personal experience that, "Jesus

You will not become priests to be served, or to lord it over others, but to serve others . . . especially the poorest of the poor, the materially poor and the spiritually poor.
POPE JOHN PAUL II
ADDRESS AT DUNWOODIE

died on the cross for me." At that point, recognizing the wonderful blessings he had received in his life through the love of the Taylor family, Keith decided to quit his job and give the Lord a year of his life in which to discern a vocation. During that year Keith lived and studied at the St.

Vincent's House of Formation in Rhode Island. In 1985, less than five years after his baptism and confirmation, Keith entered Dunwoodie to become a priest.

The four years leading up to his ordination in 1989 were filled with study, music, and apostolic work. There were also some light-hearted moments. One day he thought there was an earthquake but it was only some seminarians on the floor below rolling a bowling ball down the entire length of the hall! Keith, the convert, also learned some things in the seminary that others might take for granted: how to say the Rosary and the significance of the exposition of the Blessed Sacrament. While at Dunwoodie, the idea of an inner-city ministry started to take hold of him. Keith, looking back at his own experience as a young black man, felt that there was no door that could not be opened with a combination of faith and education.

Eight years after ordination, Father Keith, now Administrator of the Parish of St. Augustine in the South Bronx, still believes in the power of faith and education to transform lives. He takes his commitment to his community seriously. Whether it is as a role model for black youth, or as a facilitator for the adults who are learning to set goals for their parish and understand and live the meaning of Christian stewardship, Fr. Keith makes a strong statement. And sometimes it's a musical statement. Once a month his parishioners will find him with a microphone in his hand, joining the choir or taking a solo part. At St. Augustine's, liturgy is lively, the people generous, and their Administrator, Fr. Keith, very happy to have the opportunity to share with these brothers and sisters of Christ the rich blessings of the Lord.

Reverend Monsignor John Carlin, '39, Chaplain
Retired

John Carlin never intended to be a career chaplain. He entered the seminary during the Great Depression and when he left six years later, in 1939, the Second World War was underway in Europe. "It all began for us with Pearl Harbor," is how the now Msgr. Carlin begins the tale of his military career. "As I saw the young fellows being drafted and going off to the service, I'd go down to see them off at the train. I'd hear, 'Hey Father, when ya gonna join up?' So the bug hit and by '43 I asked the Cardinal. May 1, 1944, I went as a First Lieutenant to Chaplain School where I learned how to march and crawl on my belly and all that sort of thing."

Early in 1945, Father Carlin was assigned to the Philippines where his unit was preparing for the invasion of Japan. And as he tells it, "Along came August 15, a Holy Day. I had a nice announcement for the men that day, cessation of hostilities! And on my birthday, September 2, General MacArthur was up in Tokyo signing the peace treaty." World War II ended, but Father Carlin's involvement with the military chaplaincy continued until September 15, 1964, when he retired from the U.S. Air Force with the rank of Colonel.

During his twenty years of service, first with the Army Air Corps and then with the U.S. Air Force, Father Carlin saw a lot of the world. "Don't walk if you can ride; don't ride if you can fly." He loved to fly, and the map above his desk is covered with push pins representing all the places to which he has flown as he brought the sacraments to American service men and women all over the world—from the Philippines at the end of World War II, to post-war Japan and Okinawa, to Saudi Arabia in 1952, where he was the only priest within 950,000 square miles. Of Saudi he says, "I had 25 converts that year because the boys had few distractions! We had to make our own fun there. There were no U.S.O. shows. They weren't allowed to come down because they had women and Jewish entertainers. So, we did our own outdoor shows. One of the men once said, 'Chaplain, I want you to know that was the worst show I ever saw in my life!' He was serious. I said, 'Son, I want you to know that was the only show in the whole country! It was the best and the worst!'"

Father Carlin's career would take him to radar sites on the border of Canada as well as Alaska; and to the Washington, D.C., headquarters of the Air Research and Development Command, where flight technology was being developed. These were the Cold War years when Catholic theologians wrestled with the question of just war, and American servicemen sought out their chaplains for answers to their questions about the morality of nuclear warfare.

Father Carlin, an avid writer, did a turn as the Chief of the Chaplain Writers Board, Air University, Maxwell AFB, in Alabama, during an era when the threat of communism and the danger of nuclear war compelled the chaplains to develop a leadership program with the goal of impressing on the men the importance of morality.

No matter the era or the locality, whether dealing with new recruits or seasoned veterans, the gift that Father Carlin brought his men was the same. By bringing them the sacraments, he brought them back to their homes and families. "Religion is always a tie-in with home. You are putting these young men in a completely strange environment and a completely different set of clothes; is there anything connecting with all of this? Oh, yes, the parish church! So we were always known as 'Fathers' to our guys. The higher-ups would raise hell about it. 'They're suppose to call you chaplain.' 'But our guys don't call us chaplain. They are used to *Father*. It makes them feel comfortable. It makes them remember home.'"

Named a Domestic Prelate in 1962, Monsignor Carlin left the military in 1964 and continued his priestly service. He had no problem adjusting to civilian life. "I still had a commanding officer, 'Spelly', as we called him. What he said, I did." In the 33 years since his military retirement, Monsignor Carlin has served as pastor of three parishes in the Archdiocese. He is currently assisting at St. Peter's in Yonkers, doing the same thing he has done since he left Dunwoodie in 1939, bringing the sacraments to Catholic men and women, reminding them that they always have a home in Christ.   —D.M.

EXCERPTS FROM "THE HISTORIAN'S REPORT"

DELIVERED BY
BISHOP EDWIN B. BRODERICK,
PH.D., '42
CENTENNIAL ALUMNI DINNER
OCTOBER 6, 1996

*Opposite page:
Symbols of priestly
ministry from
stained glass win-
dows, Dunwoodie.*

In his light-hearted "Historian's Report" called "Dunwoodie-Revisited, 1996," the Most Rev. Edwin B. Broderick, member of the Grand Class of 1942, former Rector, and retired Bishop of Albany, walked his fellow alumni through a series of nostalgic memories that filled the room with great laughter, particularly when the joke was on him:

Last month on leaving the Academic Convocation . . . I recognized a middle-aged priest, a seminarian at the time I was Rector here. When I greeted him by name, he appeared flabbergasted as the Irish would say. He finally stammered, "Are you the BIG B?" I said, "Yes, that among many other names I do not respond to." Then he came right out with it. "Excuse me for saying this Bishop, but I thought you were dead. In fact, I remember going to your Funeral Mass." "I recall not seeing you there," I replied, "but then again I was not there either. Would you like a rain check?"

Bishop Broderick managed to tell a story that brought a chuckle to each generation of alumni gathered in the refectory that night. But the "Big B" also had a serious word for his brother priests:

What is a more fitting place than here in this big red-roofed house on Valentine Hill called by our neighbors "The Priest Factory" to give a locker room talk on vocations to the priesthood? . . .

How often we reminisce about our years spent here . . . right here where we were formed and informed about the priesthood we embraced, here where we talked and walked the loop, the quadrangle, the cloister, where we played on the ballfields and prayed in the chapel, climbing the seven-story mountain to fulfill our glorious dreams from once a lowly philosopher to that sense of wonderful accomplishment and accomplished wonderment, "Lord, why did you choose me your priest?"

. . . My plea this evening, Fathers, is not really a quest nor even a request for your financial contribution to Dunwoodie. . . . I submit that the question this evening is what must we priests do to help Dunwoodie continue as our seminary? . . . May I suggest a plan to encourage vocations? How about trying a man-to-man approach? An attempt to encourage one capable man to the priesthood and all to Dunwoodie. . . . How about trying to sell it to someone, to someone else, yes, our replacement? Remember a priest prompted and inspired many of us to the priesthood, a man we respected, admired, a role model.

. . . Frankly, Fathers, if we don't try for vocations, who else will? . . . Many of our eligibles are searching for more attractive and lucrative ways of life and lifestyles now very appealing to them. But the candidates are still out there and the Holy Spirit is in us and around us. How about warming our hands on the fire of His Spirit so as to enable us to touch others with His warmth?

We remember the hands of a priest,
anointed by God to be His hands–
folded in prayer,
raised in blessing,
outstretched in forgiveness.

Hands that feed us at the table of our Lord
and comfort us at the foot of His cross.
Hands that bathe us in living waters
and wash away our sins.

Hands that bring Glory to God
and peace to His people on earth.

We remember
the Deceased Alumni
of St. Joseph's Seminary.

The wise men followed the star, and found Christ who is Light from Light. May you too find the Lord when your pilgrimage is ended. Amen.

SOLEMN BLESSING
FOR THE FEAST OF THE EPIPHANY,
THE SACRAMENTARY

St. Joseph's Seminary A Pilgrimage of the Heart

Centennial Pilgrimage to Rome January 1-11, 1997

he experience of faith is intimately linked with the experience of places. Faith incarnate necessarily leads to physical reminders of faith and tangible experiences which foster growth in faith.

Throughout the history of religious experience, pilgrimage is understood as a time when the human person walks with and toward God in a geographic journey which mirrors a spiritual one. The spiritual effects of the journey help the pilgrim to grow closer to God and to his fellow pilgrims, both those on pilgrimage with him and those on the pilgrimage of faith which continues until the end of time.

In the middle of the centennial celebrations of St.

The whole of Christian life is like a great pilgrimage to the house of the Father . . . . This pilgrimage takes place in the heart of each person, extends to the believing community and then reaches to the whole of humanity.

POPE JOHN PAUL II
TERTIO MILLENNIO ADVENIENTE

Pope John Paul II, Feast of the Epiphany, St. Peter's Basilica.

Facing page: Detail from the stained glass lunette above the newly installed doors of the main chapel at Dunwoodie, based on the Bernini window in St. Peter's Basilica.

Joseph's Seminary, a pilgrimage comprised of 120 students, faculty, alumni and laity journeyed together to the seat of our faith, Rome. Like countless pilgrims before them, these pilgrims prepared with growing excitement for the unique experience of the catholicity of the Church afforded only in the City of Peter and Paul. Tracing the steps of the martyrs enabled them to appreciate anew the meaning of death as a witness to one's faith. Walking the same streets as the saints allowed the Dunwoodie pilgrims to experience the fulfillment of God's promise made at La Storta to Ignatius of Loyola while himself on pilgrimage to Rome: "I shall be good to you at Rome."

Assisi and Siena furthered their understanding of the tradition of Franciscan and Dominican spirituality found in the lives and writings of Francis of Assisi and Catherine of Siena. To experience those cities as they did allowed the Dunwoodie pilgrims insights into these two saints as people, themselves pilgrims.

Pilgrimage, however, is not the act of an individual, and its benefits are not limited to one's own spirituality. Early morning journeys on foot to cold Roman churches and hikes through the Umbrian and Tuscan hills forged bonds between pilgrims which nurtured a deeper appreciation of the faith shared by all.

At the beginning of our centennial year, the Holy Father urged us, "Be not afraid." Having seen, walked, touched, and lived in the places "made holy by the blood of two princes," we are not afraid, for we walk with the generations which have gone before us and the generations which will come after us as together we form the ongoing journey of the Pilgrim Church.   —E.W.

Postcards from Rome

We have walked in the footsteps of countless saints, who, with their lives, continue to inspire our vocations in the way of holiness. My only goal is to be a saint.—*Deacon Ambiorix Rodriguez* Walking into St. Peter's Basilica—this was a moment much longed for and it was an indescribable feeling. I felt welcomed into the arms of the Church, like being at home. It gave a new meaning to the idea of "being in communion with Rome." I thank the benefactors who made this pilgrimage possible. Because of their generous efforts, the Church of New York will have a number of priests whose ministry will be greatly enriched due to the experiences we have had in Rome.—*Gary DiFranco, I Theology* It has deepened my

My favorite sites were the Catacombs of St. Calistus and the Scavi beneath St. Peter's which reveal so much about the Christian faith as seen through the burials, inscriptions, and art. The celebration of the Mass in the catacombs seemed to bridge the gap between earth and the Heavenly Liturgy. The statue of the martyred St. Cecilia stands out in particular. It shows her as she was found: young, incorrupt, lying with hands bound and face covered, professing the belief in the Trinity of the Persons in the One God.
—LUKE SWEENEY, SPIRITUALITY YEAR

appreciation of the tradition of Christian art.—*Deacon Dan Greving* It became a real spiritual experience of how God has been working in the Church, throughout the ages, in a very concrete (and brick and mortar) way; and how the talents of artists have conveyed the beauty and glory of His presence among His people. I was left speechless, both by the glorious images in the Basilica and by being able to greet personally the living successor of St. Peter today. He seemed very happy to have us in his home.—*Brother Richard Roemer, C.F.R., II Theology* It was an honor and at the same time a very humbling experience to carry the prayers of the people of New York to Rome.—*Brother Stephen Norton, C.F.C., Spirituality Year* Is there any other state in the world where the stamps are sweeter to lick than Vatican

City?—*Henricus Veldkamp, III Theology* I found myself tied closer to Rome, reading the motto above the altar at St. Paul's Chapel, *Mihi Vivere Christus Est*—"For me to live is Christ"—the same motto as Dunwoodie's. Celebrating 100 years of faith with a prayer experience rooted in 2000 years of the history of our Church, transforms Dunwoodie's centennial from an anniversary to a thanksgiving for all God has granted to the Church of New York. —*Brother James Williams, S.M., I Theology*

Top left, clockwise: Fr. Edmund Whalen, faculty member and Pilgrimage organizer, explaining a point of interest; a bridge over the Tiber River; seminarian Louis Giovino with the foot of the Statue of St. Peter in St. Peter's Basilica; seminarian Henricus Veldkamp with pilgrims at the Farewell Dinner; a quiet moment in St. Peter's for seminarian Tomas Gonzalez; Statue of St. Cecilia; seminarian Frank Basset in the catacombs.

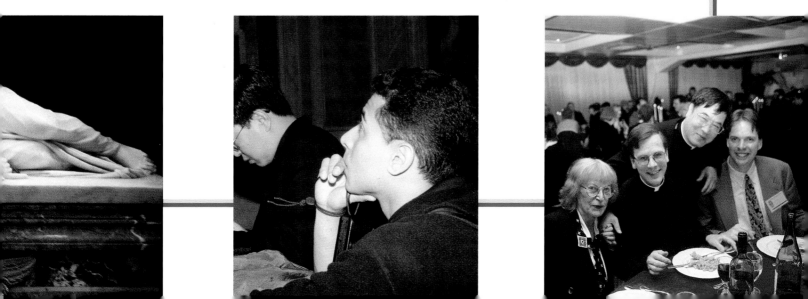

THE HEART OF NEW YORK MEETS THE HEART OF ROME

A PRIVATE AUDIENCE WITH THE HOLY FATHER

His Holiness Pope John Paul II with the Centennial Pilgrims following their private audience.

PILGRIM'S NOTES

Being in the presence of our Holy Father, Pope John Paul II, John Cardinal O'Connor and Bishop Edwin O'Brien, and the many priests and seminarians who attended our pilgrimage, I realized our common bond in the love of God and Church. Sharing this spiritual and personal time with these true servants of God made me more certain that a vocation to the priesthood is both a timeless and priceless gift. These seminarians will be our new teachers. I shall dedicate more of my time, prayer, and service for the purpose of increasing vocations to the priesthood.—*Patrick Byrne, Business Manager and volunteer at St. Patrick's Cathedral*   The second day we had a private audience with the Holy Father and it was a gift I still cannot comprehend. I shook his hand and felt his love, compassion, and joy at being with us. That night, I thought that even though it was only our second day, I could have gone home right then and would have been completely satisfied and thrilled with the trip. But the greatness of the pilgrimage continued. These days we hear much about the end of the world. This pilgrimage truly instilled in me the longevity of the Church and the incredible strength you get from true faith in God. The determination of the saints to hold fast to their faith is an inspiration to me.—*Diane Van Wagner, C.C.D. Teacher* I think the Pope has the softest hands!—*Pat Mahon, St. Joseph's Seminary Festival Choir member* So much of the trip was deeply moving for me. Many of those great moments were solitary, in the timeless peace, embraced in generations of prayer down in the chapels underneath the floor of the Basilica. I came to consider Rome a bastion and miracle of the endurance of the love of Christ. —*Patrick Clark, Artist* For 100 years St. Joseph's Seminary has prepared many extraordinary, yet humble men, chosen by God to serve his people. How blessed I was to have had the chance to meet and get acquainted with some of the current students as well as those priests who have passed through its doors and now serve the Archdiocese.—*Kevin Finegan, Human Resources Administrator* We had many opportunities to walk in the seminarians' shoes. The manner in which some of the knowledgeable professors described the many sites made history real. They brought alive the information taught from the books. By inviting the faithful along on the Centennial Pilgrimage, we had an opportunity to see for ourselves what and how the seminary is teaching its students and that they are trying to instill in them an appreciation of art history and all aspects of religious study.—*Timothy Wiggins, Pre-Theology, St. John Neumann Residence* I did not know much about the seminary before the trip. I never realized how much "school" work was involved in becoming a priest. —*Christine Brier, Teacher in Catholic Schools* For the past couple of years I have been praying for a young seminarian at the North American College who will be ordained in May. On this trip, I had the opportunity to meet and get to know him. I was very impressed with the seminarians and our priests. Their vocation is vital, and we must all encourage and nurture them. I've given St. Joseph's brochures to one of my grandsons. Who knows, maybe someday my dream of a priest in the family will be realized. It's so important for families to let their young men know that the priesthood is a very special and honorable calling. —*Ingrid Climis, St. Joseph's Festival Choir member*

CELEBRATING THE EPIPHANY WITH ST. FRANCIS OF ASSISI

We come to Assisi, now at the tomb of St. Francis, which is a place of great joy, of great peace. . . . St. Francis lived here, in this city. . . . He referred to himself as an *idiota*, as a simple man, as an ignorant man. He had a tremendous humility and from this in part, grows his deep, deep peace. So many things could be said at this altar. . . . All of us are here for this purpose of coming to know this little man, this *poverello*, this wonderful man, who changed the course of European history, and indeed, world history, by his simple life. His body is in this sarcophagus. About ten years ago they disinterred the body and examined the bones and found that he was probably 4'5", and probably died of tuberculosis and malnutrition. He had tremendous suffering and yet this is a place of great joy. He was afflicted in many ways. But he always remained joyful, filled with the praises of God—asking how can I serve, not how can I be served. I don't think that St. Francis would want us to be just like him. I don't think he would want us to return to 1209 and live the same kind of life that he lived. . . . Saint Francis would like us to be new and creative, bold, and filled with joy and peace, as we approach the third millennium in our own time. And now let us place our hearts and minds in his presence and ask him for all the graces for which he is such a great intercessor.

—Reverend John Coughlin, O.F.M., J.C.D.,
Professor of Canon Law,
from his homily at the
Tomb of St. Francis, Assisi

Top: Mass at the Tomb of St. Francis— Bishop O'Brien and Deacon Antonio Almonte; seminarians; Fr. John Coughlin

Bottom: One of the many beautiful crèches on display during the Christmas season.

SAN CLEMENTE—THE FIRST BRIDGE BETWEEN ROME AND NEW YORK

Top: Mass in San Clemente–Deacon Jeremy Hazuka reads from the Gospel; Msgr William Smith; Altar

Bottom: Some of the many architectural splendors of San Clemente.

This is an historic church and an historic place. It is ancient, it is very Roman, it is universal, and at least in one way it is personal to us. . . . It was from this church that our own diocese of New York began 189 years ago. Father Richard Concanen, O.P., was consecrated here as Bishop of New York, in the year 1808. But because Napolean's troops were in control of all the ports of Italy he spent two years trying to find a ship to take him across the Atlantic. Finally, a departure date was fixed, and that was the day he died, at age 72. Father John Connelly, also a Dominican Superior of San Clemente, finally did arrive in our diocese in November of 1815, after a voyage from Dublin that took him 67 days. Although he was the second bishop, he was the first one to take possession of our See. When he arrived in New York, there were four priests, three parishes and only 13,000 Catholics!

If you are faithful, you can be fruitful.

—Rev. Msgr. William B. Smith, S.T.D.
Professor of Moral Theology
from his homily at San Clemente

THE CARDINAL'S FAREWELL MASS FOR THE CENTENNIAL PILGRIMS

THE BASILICA OF SS. JOHN AND PAUL

Mass in the Basilica of SS. John and Paul.

Top: Cardinal O'Connor welcoming the New York pilgrims to his titular church in Rome; interior of the basilica.

Bottom: A view showing the mosaic floor in the basilica.

Facing Page: Msgr. Francis J. McAree, Vice-Rector, celebrating Mass at the Tomb of St. Pius X.

TITULAR CHURCH OF JOHN CARDINAL O'CONNOR, AND HIS TWO IMMEDIATE PREDECESSORS, FRANCIS CARDINAL SPELLMAN AND TERENCE CARDINAL COOKE

Let us enter into this holy sacrifice together, mindful that we stand here above, not simply historic ruins, but the ground drenched by the martyrs, the martyrs John and Paul. We were always told that it is the blood of the martyrs that watered the earth, that nourished the sea of the faith; so it is with great humility and a great sense of awe that we stand and repeat now the spiritual, mysterious representation of the crucifixion and the resurrection of our divine Lord. Let us pray for all those back at home, for a great increase in vocations to the priesthood and religious life in the church of New York and elsewhere throughout the United States. Let us pray for all of our families, living and deceased.

-John Cardinal O'Connor,

from his homily at SS. John and Paul

CENTENNIAL PILGRIMAGE
CLOSING MASS AT ST. PETER'S BASILICA
TOMB OF ST. PIUS X, PATRON OF PRIESTS

As we come to the end of our pilgrimage to this holy city of Rome and to the other holy places, we find ourselves filled with many emotions. The emotion of gratitude, certainly, gratitude to God for our Catholic faith and the blessings of this trip. . . . Along with gratitude we are also filled with wonder, wonder at the depth of our Catholic tradition as its historical grandeur becomes evident in the majestic basilicas and monuments which we have seen.

Some of us might also have reflected on what we are taking back with us from this trip. Calories? Yes. Mementos? Yes. New friendships, and perhaps, deepened ones? Yes. Most importantly, however, our pilgrimage is allowing us to take back one very special thing; and that is a renewed sense of who God wants us to be.

This sense of renewal is certainly one of our Holy Father's intentions for all of us as we approach the new millennium. Quite fittingly, it was also the intention of the saint at whose tomb we celebrate this Mass on the day of our departure. Pope St. Pius X said at the beginning of his pontificate that he wanted to renew all things in Christ. He is known as a patron of priests because of his concern for the spiritual life, his wish to carry out the reform of seminaries, and his personal sense of the importance of a simple life devoted to following the example of Jesus. His own life was an example of how humility and grandeur can be both contrasting and complementary. . . . Pius X knew that true grandeur was not found in externals but in the humility of the servant who made Christ so visible to the world. . . .

All of the magnificent basilicas we have seen tell us of this. They are grand, not just because of their size or the beautiful works of art they contain, but instead for the saint on whom they are centered, whether Francis of Assisi, Clare, Catherine of Siena, or Peter in this marvelous basilica. All of these great saints knew and lived the wisdom that John the Baptist proclaimed to all, that they must decrease while He, the Savior, must increase. . . . Let this wisdom be the great treasure that we take home from this pilgrimage, the treasure of a renewed sense of who God wants us to be.

May this pilgrimage always remind us that true grandeur lies in humility. May we live what we have learned, and may the name of our Lord Jesus Christ be praised both now and forever! Amen. . .

—Reverend Monsignor Francis J. McAree, S.T.D.
Vice-Rector, St. Joseph's Seminary

The liturgy, as the summit and source of the Church's existence and in particular of all Christian prayer, plays an influential and indispensable role in the pastoral work of promoting vocations. . . . Every liturgical celebration, and especially the Eucharist, reveals to us the true face of God and grants us a share in the paschal mystery, in the "hour" for which Jesus came into the world and toward which he freely and willingly made his way in obedience to the Father's call.

POPE JOHN PAUL II
PASTORES DABO VOBIS

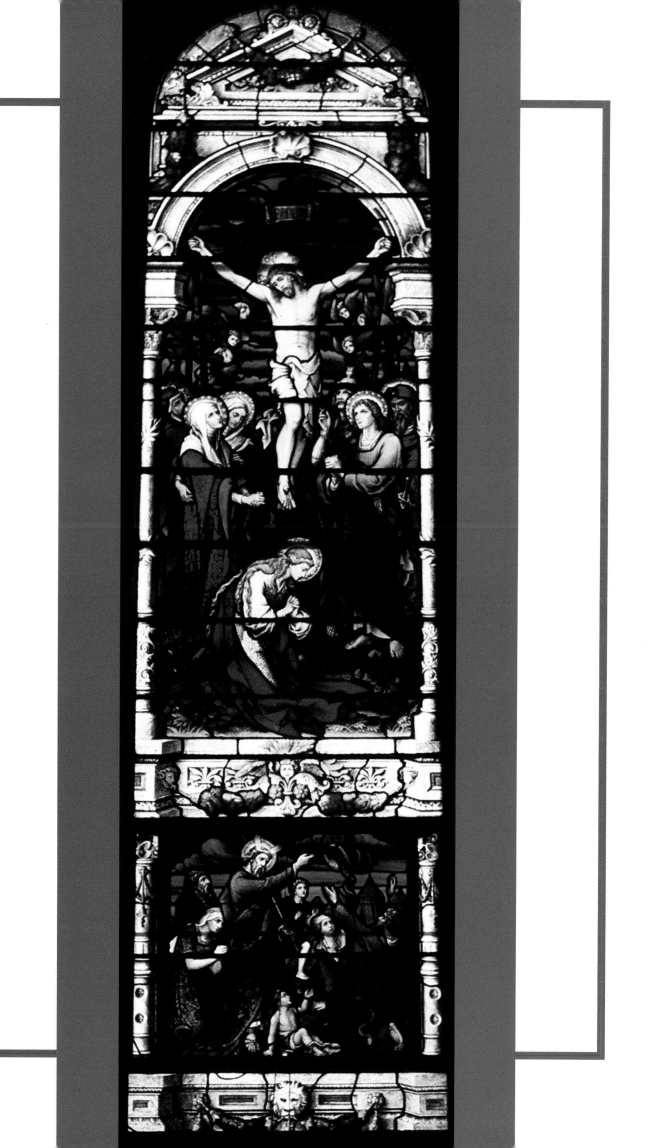

*The Heart of the
Church of New York 1896-1996*

St. Joseph's Seminary "Come and See."

Vocation Day Mass March 25, 1997

The time has come to speak courageously about priestly life as a priceless gift and a splendid and privileged form of Christian living.

Pope John Paul II
PASTORES DABO VOBIS

man kneels before his Archbishop robed in the liturgical vestments of priesthood for the first time. The hands of the Archbishop hold the chalice and paten brought to him by members of the congregation. As the ordinand touches the sacred vessels held by his Shepherd, he hears the words: "Accept from the people of God the gifts to be offered to him. Know what you are doing, and imitate the mystery you celebrate; model your life on the mystery of the Lord's cross." The mystery celebrated is, in fact, the Eucharist which is modeled on the Paschal Mystery—Christ's passion, death and resurrection.

How does a young man arrive at this point in his human life, ready to imitate such a mystery? In 1979, Pope John Paul II reaffirmed an insight which helps answer these questions. Speaking to youth at Madison Square Garden in New York he proclaimed, "When you wonder about the mystery of yourself, look to Christ who gives you the meaning of life." The Holy Father's wisdom challenges young men to "look to Christ" for the answer to their vocation. This "looking" forms a foundation for knowing the Lord and prepares a man to imitate Christ, the High Priest. Of course, it is God who initiates the call to the priesthood, yet by prayerfully looking to Jesus, a man begins to understand the meaning of a vocation. As grace operates in a man's heart, it draws forth a free response and a generous, sacrificial offering to serve the Church as a priest.

Wonderfully, the Church offers the pillars of Sacred Scripture and the Eucharist to help men discern the truth of their vocation. A man utilizes these pillars to discover if God desires him to accept the priesthood as his life's mission. In the Gospel of John a man reads the story of the first disciples and begins to understand the nature of a priestly vocation. "As John the Baptist watched Jesus walk by he said, 'Look! There is the Lamb of God!' The two disciples heard what he said, and followed Jesus. When Jesus turned around and noticed them following him, he asked them, 'What are you looking for?' They said to him, 'Rabbi, where do you stay?' 'Come and see,' he answered" (John 1:36-39).

The Eucharist is the center of the priest's existence and the wellspring of the Church's sacramental life. It is in the Blessed Sacrament, through sacramental communion, liturgical celebration and eucharistic prayer, that the young heart encounters Christ and "stays" in His midst to learn of a call to priestly service. The meaning of the Eucharist, perfectly reflected in the cross of Christ, teaches the Church the value of sacrifice. Thus, as Christ gave His body and shed His blood, so the priest is called to give his life as an offering to the Father for the sake of the Church. Planted by the Holy Spirit and nurtured by family and parish, a vocation to the priesthood is gradually discerned by a man who decides to imitate the mystery of the Eucharist and to model his life on the mystery of the Lord's cross.

—R.McK.

Opposite page: Crucifixion of Christ, detail from a stained glass window in the Chapel of SS. Peter and Paul, Dunwoodie. The full window, on the previous page, pairs the image of Christ's Crucifixion with that of Moses Raising the Bronze Serpent on a Stake.

This page: Young men from Cathedral Preparatory Seminary attending the Chrism Mass.

> *Let us pray that God our almighty Father will bless this oil so that all who are anointed with it may be inwardly transformed and come to share in eternal salvation.*
> FROM *THE CHRISM MASS*

AS PRIESTS RENEW THEIR COMMITMENT AT THE CHRISM MASS, THE CARDINAL ASKS OTHERS TO CONSIDER THE CALL

Students from Cathedral Preparatory Seminary, Rye, and the St. John Neumann Residence, Riverdale, Bronx, joined the seventy other young and older men present considering a vocation to the priesthood, at the Chrism Mass on March 25, at St. Patrick's Cathedral, at which hundreds of priests from the Archdiocese renewed their commitment to the priesthood. Several of the prospective priests had attended one of the four vocation retreats given by Cardinal O'Connor and some had already had the chance to learn about the Neumann Residence during an Open House held the previous week.

Cardinal O'Connor was the principal

celebrant at the annual Mass which commemorates the "birthday of the priesthood," when Jesus instituted the Eucharist at the Last Supper. The Cardinal asked prospective candidates to the priesthood to join in spirit with the priests as they pledged their renewal of priestly commitment, and to begin thinking more seriously about God's call. "It has never been easy to be a priest," he said. "You cannot hope even to consider serving our Divine Lord as a priest unless you're prepared to lay aside everything else."

Noting that the Feast of the Annunciation would normally be celebrated March 25, if the date did not come during Holy Week, the Cardinal said that the priesthood received its beginning with Mary's "Yes" to the angel. Her obedience brought forth the Savior who is the great High Priest. "God may be waiting for your will," he told the men. "He never forces you but He does demand, 'If you want to follow me . . . .' It takes a real man to do this."   —B.C.

Top, left to right: Cardinal John O'Connor greeting youth during the Chrism Mass; bishops, priests and acolytes processing in through the doors of St. Patrick's Cathedral.

Bottom, left to right: Scenes from the Chrism Mass.

89

Discerning the Priesthood— A Call and an Invitation

When asked about his desire to pursue a priestly vocation, George Sears, fourth-year student at Cathedral Preparatory Seminary speaks of a *calling* and an *invitation*. He has no doubt that this was a decision God made for him. He credits his family, the example of priests and his teachers, however, for *inviting* him to realize this calling: *My enthusiasm for my religion did not come from thin air, but was rooted in the example of my mother. She has always been an example of holiness; an inspiration to me. Since I was a baby my mother taught me how to stay in touch with God. Mom always says: "Jesus is your best friend."*

At church George met Father Failla, *a great big bear of a man with a smile on his face. He always gave me a hug when I saw him, and he took the time to see how I was doing. He has a great influence on me to this day; whenever I think of a priest, I think of someone happy.*

George is quick to point out that while the example of his mother and Father Failla kept the priesthood on his mind, it was the principal of his grammar school who encouraged him to explore the idea more fully: *She told me about a high school for young men considering the priesthood. So I visited Cathedral Prep. It took me all of two minutes to decide that this was where I would spend the next four years of my life.*

In his four years at the Prep, George has taken the usual Catholic high school academic courses. He has lived at the Bishop Ford Residence, located in a wing of St. Joseph's Seminary. This experience has given him a taste of the seminary system: *We are able to learn more about the path to priesthood through the fine examples set by our older brother seminarians and the faculty of St. Joseph's Seminary.* Speaking of the priests at the Prep, George says: *Their dedication to the students is truly inspiring. However, they also know how to have a good time while living holy lives.*

In the fall, George will continue in the seminary system when he enters the St. John Neumann Residence where he will live and study while attending college. After Neumann, his goal is to attend St. Joseph's Seminary and fulfill his dream of becoming a priest. When his time comes to be ordained, a lifetime of discernment will be fulfilled. What will he be thinking about when he celebrates his first Mass? *I will look back on the education, the experiences and the people who made me what I have become. Without these individuals, and a call from God, I would never have become a priest; I would never have realized my dream.*

—D.M. with G.S.

*Y*ou must enter into an intimate relationship with the Holy Spirit
and with all His gifts, in order that the Lord's intentions
for you may become clear. This is another way of expressing the need
for wisdom. Indeed, the seminary must be a school of wisdom.
Here you must live with your patron, St. Joseph, and with Mary, the
mother of Jesus; and in the silence of this intimacy you
will learn that wisdom of which St. Luke speaks: "Jesus for his part
progressed steadily in wisdom and age and grace before God and men."

POPE JOHN PAUL II
ADDRESS AT DUNWOODIE

Opposite page: Fourth-year Cathedral Prep student George Sears with his mother in the school chapel.
This page: Christ Crucified, detail from a crucifix in the St. John Neumann Residence.

Accept this Easter candle.
May it always dispel
        the darkness of this night!
May the Morning Star
        which never sets
find this flame still burning:
Christ, that Morning Star,
who came back from the dead,
and shed his peaceful light
        on all mankind,
your son who lives and reigns
        for ever and ever.
            Amen.

FROM THE *EXSULTET*
THE EASTER PROCLAMATION
THE SACRAMENTARY

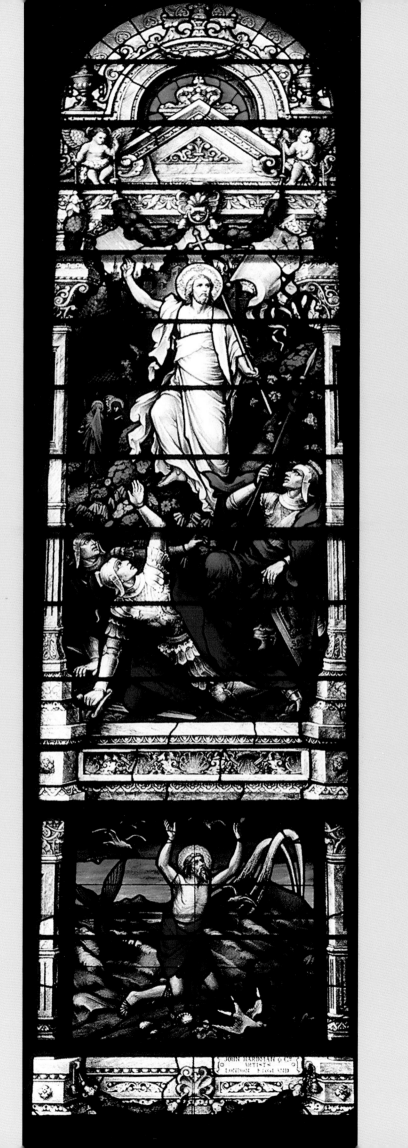

St. Joseph's Seminary Proclaims the Risen Christ!

EXSULTET!
Easter Concert of Sacred Music
April 6, 1997

ight truly blessed when heaven is wedded to earth and man is reconciled with God.

If St. Joseph's Seminary is the heart of the Church in New York, the chapel of the seminary has been the heart of the heart. The main chapel of SS. Peter and Paul is the center and crown of Dunwoodie. Adorned with an Italian mosaic floor, oak choir stalls, brilliant stained glass, a Casavant Frères organ, frescoes, historical and precious vesture, vessels and appointments, it is the locus of a vibrant liturgical spirituality. One of the jewels in that crown is the sacred music that daily fills this sacred space.

The place of sacred music in the life of the church has an effective function and a lofty purpose. Its function is to be the handmaiden of the liturgy, making the sung prayers beautiful, solemn, and moving. The lofty purpose of sacred music, like the liturgy itself, was described most succinctly by Pope St. Pius X when he said that the purpose of sacred music was "the glory of God and the sanctification and edification of the faithful."

For one hundred years, sacred music has been an integral and vibrant part of St. Joseph's Seminary. The resonance of our main chapel has brought to life a brilliant repertoire performed by generations of seminarians and priests who have lifted their

voices in prayer. Each seminarian is invited to move from the technique of making music to the joy of blending mind and voice in song. From 1896 to the present, each visitor can delight in chanting at the Liturgy of the Hours, the careful preparation of Gregorian chant, the heavenly Roman polyphony and hymns sung by choir and *schola*, the timbres of the organ leading and accompanying worship, and, most recently, the sounds of many and varied instruments for liturgy and concert to delight the contemporary ear.

"Night truly blessed when heaven is wedded to earth and man is reconciled with God." This text, from the *Exsultet,* the Easter Proclamation, is a fitting reminder of what sacred music tries to do when it weds sacred text with music. The Eucharist is the place where heaven is wedded to earth. The celebration of the Eucharist, and by extension, the Adoration of the Blessed Sacrament and the Liturgy of the Hours, are the center of our seminary life. The music prepared for each celebration is our attempt to offer our human genius as a sacrifice of praise to our God.

The prayer and liturgy of the seminary community and all who have come and will come to worship in our chapel create the union and communion that is at the heart of our worship—the glory of God and the sanctification and edification of God's people.

—A.S.

Rejoice, heavenly powers!
Sing, choirs of angels!
Exult, all creation around God's throne!
Jesus Christ, our king, is risen!
Sound the trumpet of salvation!
FROM THE *EXSULTET*

This page: Exsultet! brought together the talents of the Seminary Choir, the Centennial Concert Choir, Schola Cantorum, and Orchestra, in an Easter concert of sacred music at the Performing Arts Center at S.U.N.Y., Purchase.

Opposite page: The Resurrection of Christ, detail from a stained glass window in the SS. Peter and Paul Chapel, Dunwoodie. The full window, seen on the previous page, pairs this New Testament image with the Old Testament's Jonah Coming Forth from the Mouth of the Whale.

Exsultet

An Easter Concert of Sacred Music

[sheet music notation]

St. Joseph's Seminary's
Centennial Celebration

On April 6, St. Joseph's Seminary took its tradition of sacred music to the Concert Hall at the Performing Arts Center at the State University of New York in Purchase for a very simple reason, as Bishop Edwin F. O'Brien explains in the concert program: "The venerable walls of our beloved Seminary are unable to contain the numbers who will enjoy *Exsultet!*" Indeed, over 2,000 enthusiastic supporters of Dunwoodie turned out for the Easter Concert—a musical touch to the seminary's centennial celebration. Father Anthony Sorgie, Ed.D., Academic Dean and Director of Sacred Music at the seminary, remarked that it would take several performances in the main chapel at Dunwoodie to accommodate as many people. Part of the chapel, however, did accompany the performers to

the concert hall: The Paschal Candle, lovingly carried from the seminary's chapel of SS. Peter and Paul, burned brightly on the stage as a silent reminder of the glorious faith proclaimed that day by the combined forces of the choristers, musicians and the Center's Flentrop pipe organ, one of the largest portable organs in the world.

The *Exsultet*, the Easter Proclamation, sung by the Seminary Choir, was broken into five parts in order to form the thematic backdrop for the concert and introduce the treasures of Easter music sung by the Centennial Concert Choir, a group of ninety-six singers representing more than thirty-five parishes in the Archdiocese. In the concert program, Father Sorgie explains the purpose behind bringing all these performers together: "We are approaching the Third Millennium and the Christian community has given to the Church a wealth of music composed for the feasts of the Paschal Mystery. Through the chants and polyphony of the Liturgy, soloists' arias, orchestral masterpieces, and organ works, composers ancient and modern have helped to proclaim: Christ Has Died, Christ Is Risen, Christ Will Come Again!"

Bishop O'Brien compared the voices of the men and women of the choir to those of the Apostles, whose blended voices, raised in proclamation of the risen Lord, made "for a convincing Christian community."

Sacred text, Christian witness, and human artistry have always built communities: in the cathedral, in the monastery, in the seminary, and even here—on stage—at S.U.N.Y., Purchase. –D.M.

Top, left to right:
Bishop Edwin O'Brien
addressing the audience;
Soloists Wayne Neuzil,
baritone, and Douglas
Jabara, tenor;
Father Sorgie conducting.
Some of the men and
women of the Centennial
Concert Choir.

Bottom left to right:
Concert rehearsal at
S.U.N.Y., Purchase;
Centennial Concert
Organists, Robert S.
Harvey, and seminarian,
George Hafemann;
Choristers;
The Paschal Candle—
brought from
Dunwoodie.

Rejoice, O earth,
in shining splendor,
radiant in the brightness
of your King!
Christ has conquered!
Glory fills you!
Darkness vanishes forever!
FROM THE *EXSULTET*

A PRECIOUS GIFT

One of the seminary's prized possessions is this cross, a gift of Pope Leo XIII, supreme pontiff at the time of the dedication of St. Joseph's Seminary.

His portrait, at Dunwoodie, is one of the only portraits showing a pontiff smiling.

A photograph from 1947 shows the cross atop a side altar. Today it can be found on the reredos, as seen on page 100.

the marble of the two side altars. Its mensa is a single slab of Italian marble weighing 3,000 pounds.

Notable restorations included the refinishing of the mural in the apse and the removal of the fourth row of seating on each side of the nave, which had been added in 1913. Extensive repair work to the marble flooring was required in order to restore the seating arrangement to its original design. The overall effect of the 1983 renovations left the chapel cleaner, brighter and in keeping with the liturgical norms established by the Second Vatican Council. Sadly, Cardinal Cooke did not live long enough to see the completion of this work. His successor, then-Archbishop John Joseph O'Connor, presided over the solemn dedication on October 16, 1984.

—Adapted from, *The History of the Chapel
of St. Joseph's Seminary*

This page, top: Easter Vigil, 1997, shows the Chapel of SS. Peter and Paul as it appears today.

Opposite page, top: Pope John Paul II, Chapel of SS. Peter and Paul, October 6, 1995.

Opposite page, bottom: Portrait of Terence Cardinal Cooke, generous benefactor of the Chapel's restoration and renovation, from Dunwoodie.

This page, bottom: Construction of the new altar of sacrifice, 1983.

On August 12, 1896, New York's Archbishop Michael Augustine Corrigan dedicated the new diocesan seminary at Dunwoodie. Among its many fine appointments was a splendid new organ, the first of three instruments that would successively reside high in the east gallery of the Chapel of Saints Peter and Paul.

The first organ was built by the venerable firm of John Henry and Caleb Sherwood Odell, founded in 1859. On November 30, 1895, the firm signed a contract with the "Most Reverend M.A. Corrigan," promising to deliver an organ "of the best material" by July 1, 1896. The agreed price was $3,600, payable upon completion of the instrument.

The Odell served the seminary well during the early part of the new century. By the late 1930s, however, the seminary's financial situation was such that the maintenance of the organ could not be kept up. The Odells had continued to service the instrument though the years, but, since money was unavailable for repairs, they would simply disconnect what could not be fixed, until the organ was nearly unplayable.

By 1942, it was clear that the disrepair of the organ needed to be addressed. Francis Cardinal Spellman, who had become the Archbishop of New York in 1939, moved quickly on a proposal to install a replacement in the chapel. A new instrument was completely out of the question due to the war effort, but the Atlas Organ Company, a small Bronx repair firm, had an instrument that would do. This organ served the seminary through the war years and beyond. But, by the mid-1950s, it was in bad condition, and the Odells, who serviced it, advised that something be done fairly soon.

In 1947, Msgr. Richard B. Curtin, '42, Director of Music at the seminary since the previous year, was appointed to head the Archdiocesan Commission on Church Music. This brought him in contact with many organ builders, among them, the respected Canadian firm of Casavant Frères. Msgr. Curtin suggested that an entirely new organ be built for the seminary. Casavant offered to build an instrument for a price under $35,000. With the approval of Msgr. Francis Reh, then rector, a contract was signed, and the new organ was scheduled for delivery in 1960.

Among the documents to come out of the Second Vatican Council were several addressing the arrangement of the church building. The organ and other lawfully approved musical instruments should be located where they can support both choral and congregational singing and also be heard properly when played alone. Since moving the organ was out of the question, Msgr. Curtin decided to experiment by placing a second console at the front of the chapel. The result was successful enough that Msgr. Curtin, using money raised from recordings of the seminary choir, contracted to build a permanent console, which was installed on the north side of the sanctuary.

REDEDICATION

The organ had served admirably for more than twenty years when, in 1983, the chapel was restored under the guidance of Terence Cardinal Cooke. Throughout the late 1980s, periodic maintenance was done on the organ. In 1986, Fr. Anthony D. Sorgie, '82, was appointed Director of Music, filling the position that Msgr. Curtin had left some 20 years earlier. During his tenure, the organ has received a wide audience through the annual Advent-Christmas Concert. It may also be heard on the two compact disc recordings issued by the seminary: the 1993 Advent-Christmas Concert and "A Treasury of Sacred Music," featuring music recorded at the seminary between the 1950s and 1995.

By the early 1990s, the organ had begun to show signs of age. Since the seminary would be celebrating its centennial in 1996, it was determined that a restoration of the organ would be one of the projects undertaken in anticipation of this milestone.

Msgr. Curtin and Fr. Sorgie served as co-directors of the project and began the preparation in early 1995. Since Casavant was still building quality instruments, it was only logical that they should perform the work. On June 21, 1995, a contract was signed between St. Joseph's Seminary and Casavant Frères. The complete project, including a new three-manual console in the chancel, cost $128,115. The money was raised through the "Organ Restoration Program," which received 444 gifts of all sizes in the space of four months.

The following months were busy ones for the seminary. On October 6, Dunwoodie was graced with a visit by the Holy Father, Pope John Paul II, at which time the organ was heard by millions through the extensive radio and television coverage of that historic event. Shortly after the 1995 Advent-Christmas Concert, the reed stops, the Positive Cymbel, and a number of other pipes were removed to Canada for repairs.

Finally, on June 4, 1996, all of the new and restored pipes, as well as the new console, arrived at the seminary. The organ's debut, however, was somewhat bittersweet: the Mass of Christ, the High Priest, celebrated for Fr. Brian P. Barrett, '84, a member of the faculty, who died unexpectedly on July 13.

While the Casavant plays organ literature of all schools with a certain authenticity, perhaps its greatest claim to fame will always be its service, day in and day out, to the spiritual, liturgical, and musical formation of the seminarians. For almost forty years, this instrument has led the community in praising God through song, a duty which it will faithfully continue in Dunwoodie's second century of service to the Church.

—G.H.

Most of us have heard the organ called "the King of Instruments." Do you know who first said it? Wolfgang Amadeus Mozart. In a letter to his father Leopold in October, 1777, he wrote: "In my eyes and ears, the organ will ever be the King of Instruments."

Mozart's evaluation becomes valuable when we realize how competent he was to make it. In his short lifetime he had composed for just about every kind of instrument he could find, so we respect his naming the pipe organ the King. In the same vein, Robert Schumann, almost a century later, called the organ the "Royal Instrument," and *Grove's Dictionary of Music and Musicians* says it is "that great triumph of human skill . . . the most perfect musical instrument."

But what about the all-time master of the organ, Johann Sebastian Bach, the greatest composer for the instrument, the greatest performer and probably the finest evaluator as well? To my knowledge he never wrote anything about the instrument, but he had much to say about the purpose of the music he composed for it and played on it. Regularly, the title page of his compositions carried the simple dedication, "To the Glory of Almighty God," and the last page was usually marked: "*Fine. S.D.Gl.*" — *Soli Deo Gloria.* He knew what the organ and its music were for. He knew that the instrument had been a vehicle of worship for hundreds of years before his time, that it had literally "grown up" in the church.

If Bach were alive today, he would marvel at the technical advances made in building pipe organs, and he would explain again that its purpose is the glory of Almighty God. He would tell how it enables men and women to praise God by supporting their sung praise, by enhancing the majesty of their ceremonies, by inspiring thoughts of God's beauty in their meditation, by uplifting spirits that may flag, by consoling souls that sometimes hurt, by encouraging further ardor in hearts that want to love. Bach would be pleased to point out that the organ is the only musical instrument mentioned in any church document, ancient or modern, as a means of praising God.

In the Latin Church, the pipe organ is to be held in high esteem, for it is the traditional musical instrument which adds wonderful splendor to the Church's ceremonies and powerfully lifts up man's mind to God and to higher things.

VATICAN II
SACROSANCTUM CONCILIUM

A HEAVENLY COLLABORATION:
A TREASURY OF SACRED MUSIC

The 100th anniversary of St. Joseph's Seminary provided the occasion to assemble this anthology of sacred music which features five decades of seminary voices. Selections from the original reference recordings and master tapes made by Msgr. Curtin in the 1950s and 1960s have been remastered using state-of-the-art digital technology.

In the summer of 1995, Fr. Sorgie formed the Centennial Choir, inviting priest alumni of Dunwoodie to join the seminarians for a unique recording session. The membership of this choir represents the ordination classes spanning 1978 through 2000. The rich one-hundred-year muscial heritage of St. Joseph's Seminary, performed by fifty years of Dunwoodie men, is captured for all ages on one recording. The result is a supreme example of the collaborative work of the Church in the modern world.

The Catholic Church, by her nature, is on a mission to speak the saving message of Jesus Christ in many languages and various media. With an abiding understanding of this truth, St. Joseph's Seminary now sends into the world the sacred words and tones which form its life of prayer — prayer which forms priests of tomorrow who will lead the People of God in their pilgrimage here on earth.

—B.C./*CNY*

A Treasury of Sacred Music

Saint Joseph's Seminary

Msgr. Curtin, Bishop O'Brien, and Fr. Sorgie, following the Exsultet! concert; seminary recordings: Msgr. Curtin's L.P.'s of the seminary choirs under his direction and Fr. Sorgie's C.D.'s, featuring the Seminarian Choir, the Festival Choir, and the Centennial Choir.

Opposite page, top: Bishop Edwin O'Brien, at the organ rededication ceremony.

Opposite page, bottom: Donald Dumler, principal organist at Saint Patrick's Cathedral, performing during the ceremony.

Full authority has been given to me
both in heaven and on earth;
go, therefore, and make disciples of all nations.

Baptize them in the name of the Father,
and of the Son,
and of the Holy Spirit.

Teach them to carry out everything I
have commanded you.
And know that I am with you always,
until the end of the world!

MATTHEW 28:18-20

St. Joseph's Seminary Living the Mystery

Ordination to the Sacred Priesthood May 17, 1997

"What is a priest without love?" Cardinal O'Connor asked in his address to the eight men he ordained to the priesthood May 17, the day before Pentecost. Noting the divisions in the Church, he stressed that only love which comes from the Holy Spirit, and the peace that flows from it, could gather differing factions together as one Body in Christ.

The eight men, who had been previously ordained to the diaconate, made their promise of obedience before the Cardinal and lay prostrate on the sanctuary floor of St. Patrick's Cathedral as the Litany of Saints was chanted. They knelt for the Cardinal to lay his hands upon each of them, followed by four bishops and more than 100 priests. They then were vested as

Live the mystery
*that has been placed
in your hands.*
Pope John Paul II
PASTORES DABO VOBIS

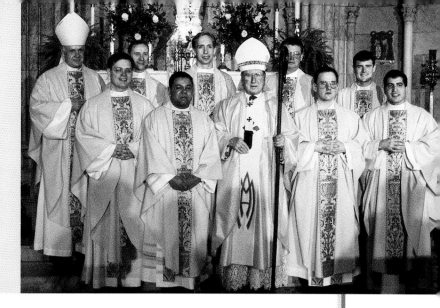

priests, had their hands anointed, and were presented with a paten and chalice signifying their mandate to offer the sacrifice of the Mass. They did just that a few moments later when they joined the Cardinal, bishops and priests in the Liturgy of the Eucharist.

The ordination was the culmination of as many as eight years of preparation for some of the new priests. They had spent two to four years at the St. John Neumann Residence. Most had studied four years of theology at Dunwoodie; one had been sent to the North American College in Rome. The long road to the priesthood was summed up when the eight raised their hands at the consecration and joined the Cardinal in saying, *This is My Body, This is the cup of My Blood.* Immediately after Mass, they brought the gift of their priesthood to the people as they stood at stations about the cathedral and offered first blessings to parents, relatives, and friends. The people who had nurtured and supported their vocations through the years received the first fruits of the new priests' faithful response to God's call.

Such a response, extraordinary under any circumstances, is especially notable in a day when the priesthood is often ill-depict-ed or maligned. Amid great challenges, the eight men will also have the joy and consolation of serving a Church and a world that are in desperate need of priests. Only a priest can forgive sins, only a priest can offer the Eucharist, only a priest can give God's parting pardon to the dying in the Sacrament of Anointing. The parish will love them because they are priests; and even older folks will call them, "Father." They will be held to a higher standard and be sought out not as other men, but as men called by God.

"It is love that you should strive for," the Cardinal exhorted the young men. "Love one another. Love your brother priests in the Church of New York. Love God's people equally. We can take ourselves as human beings too seriously, but we can never take our priesthood too seriously."

—B.C.

Opposite page, top: Mr. and Mrs. William Dillon, parents of the newly ordained Father Robert Dillon.

Opposite page, bottom: Jesus Appears after the Resurrection, detail from a stained glass window in chapel of SS. Peter and Paul, Dunwoodie. The full window, seen on the previous page, is paired with the image of the High Priest offering the Sacrifice in the Holy of Holies, from the Old Testament; Chalice, detail from a stained glass window in the Chapel of SS. Peter and Paul, Dunwoodie.

This page, top: Cardinal John O'Connor and Archbishop Edwin O'Brien with the newly ordained class of 1997.

THE HOMILY

This man, your relative and friend, is now to be raised to the order of priests. Consider carefully the position to which he is to be promoted in the Church.

It is true that God has made his entire people a royal priesthood in Christ. But our High Priest, Jesus Christ, also chose some of his followers to carry out publicly in the Church a priestly ministry in his name on behalf of mankind. . . .

Our brother has seriously considered this step

EXAMINATION ⊙F THE CANDIDATE

My son, before you proceed to the Order of the Presbyterate, declare before the people your intention to undertake this priestly office. Are you resolved, with the help of the Holy Spirit, to discharge without fail the Office of Priesthood in the presbyteral order as a conscientious fellow worker with the bishops in caring for the Lord's flock?

I am.

Are you resolved to celebrate the mysteries of Christ faithfully and religiously as the Church has handed them down to us for the glory of God and the sanctification of Christ's people?

I am.

Are you resolved to exercise the ministry of the word worthily and wisely, preaching the Gospel and explaining the Catholic faith?

I am.

Are you resolved to consecrate your life to God for the salvation of his people, and to unite yourself more closely every day to Christ the High Priest, who offered himself for us to the Father as a perfect sacrifice?

I am, with the help of God.

PR⊙MISE ⊙F ⊙BEDIENC

Do you promise respect and obedience to me and my successors?

I do.

May God who has begun the good work in yo bring it to fulfillment.

d is now to be ordained to priesthood in the
esbyteral order. He is to serve Christ the
eacher, Priest, and Shepherd in his ministry
hich is to make his own body, the Church,
ow into the people of God, a holy temple. . . .

y son, you are now to be advanced to the
der of the presbyterate. . . . Share with all
ankind the word of God you have received
th joy. Meditate on the law of God, believe
hat you read, teach what you believe, and put
to practice what you teach. . . .

THE LITANY OF THE SAINTS

Lord, have mercy.
Lord, have mercy.
Christ, have mercy.
Christ, have mercy.
Lord, have mercy.
Lord, have mercy.

Hear us, Lord our God,
and pour out upon this servant of yours
the blessing of the Holy Spirit
and the grace and power of the priesthood.
In your sight we offer this man for ordination:
support him with your unfailing love.

We ask this through Christ our Lord.
Amen.

111

LAYING ON OF HANDS

FIRST BLESSING

Always remember
the example of the
Good Shepherd who
came not to be
served but to serve. . . .

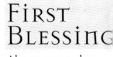

PRAYER OF CONSECRATION

Come to our help,
Lord, holy Father, almighty and eternal God;
you are the source of every honor and dignity,
of all progress and stability. . . .

In the desert
you extended the spirit of Moses to seventy wise men
who helped him to rule the great company of his people.
You shared among the sons of Aaron
the fullness of their father's power,
to provide worthy priests in sufficient number
for the increasing rites of sacrifice and worship.
With the same loving care
you gave companions to your Son's apostles
to help in teaching the faith:
they preached the Gospel to the whole world. . . .

Almighty Father,
grant to this servant of yours
the dignity of priesthood.
Renew within him the Spirit of holiness. . . .

INVESTITURE WITH STOLE AND CHASUBLE

May he be faithful in working with the order of bishops,
so that the words of the Gospel may reach the ends of the earth,
and the family of nations,
made one in Christ,
may become God's one, holy people.

We ask this through our Lord Jesus Christ, your Son,
who lives and reigns with you and the Holy Spirit,
one God, for ever and ever.

Amen.

Kiss of Peace

Peace be with you.
And also with you.

Presentation of Gifts

Accept from the holy people of God
the gifts to be offered to him.
Know what you are doing,
and imitate the mystery you celebrate:
model your life on the mystery
of the Lord's cross.

Anointing of Hands

The Father anointed our Lord Jesus Christ
through the power of the Holy Spirit.
May Jesus preserve you to sanctify the Christian people
and to offer sacrifice to God.

—Text from the *Ordination of Deacons, Priests, and Bishops*

St. Joseph's Seminary — Opening the Door to the Next 100 Years

At the beginning of this commemorative book we were reminded of the words of Our Holy Father Pope John Paul II during his visit to St. Joseph's Seminary when he told us: "The wisdom of the Cross is at the heart of the life and ministry of every priest." The stained glass window pictured at the left speaks of the self-offering of Jesus to the Father, an action accomplished on the Cross and made present to us each time the Eucharist is celebrated.

The priest as celebrant of the Eucharist allows the salvific effects of this sacrifice to continue in the world and so, the eucharistic ministry of the priest is the heart of the matter. From this ministry all else takes its life and meaning. In light of this we have not been hesitant to echo the words of our Archbishop, John Cardinal O'Connor, and speak of this seminary as the "Heart of the Church in New York."

Pope John Paul II has spoken of the year 2000

as a Jubilee. Our Centennial Year has also had the character of a Jubilee Year, a year of favor from the Lord. An Archdiocesan Family Day, Academic Convocation, Alumni Mass and Dinner, Pilgrimage to Rome, Centennial Vocation Mass in St. Patrick's Cathedral, Easter Concert at S.U.N.Y., Purchase, N.Y., all leading up to our Centennial Mass and Dinner on October 4, 1997, have each been valuable and beautiful moments leading us to a deeper appreciation of the mission, heritage and strength of St. Joseph's Seminary, Dunwoodie.

We believe that the future is filled with hope. With God's help and yours we will now begin to provide Priests for the New Millennium. We close this book with a prayer that Our Lord Jesus Christ will continue to bless our work as we open the door to the next one hundred years. . .

—Reverend Monsignor Francis J. McAree
Rector, St. Joseph's Seminary, Dunwoodie

ПOTES

ABBREVIATIONS

AA   *Apostolicam Actuositatem* (Decree on the Apostolate of the Laity, Vatican II)

DHSJS *Dunwoodie: The History of St. Joseph's Seminary, Yonkers, New York* by Thomas J. Shelley

HJSJ   *The History of St. Joseph's Seminary of New York.* Cathedral Library Association

OT   *Optatam Totius* (Decree on Priestly Training, Vatican II)

PDV   John Paul II, Apostolic Exhortation. *Pastores dabo vobis*, 25 March 1992

RM   *The Sacramentary* (Roman Missal)

RO   *Rite of Ordination of Deacons, Priests, and Bishops*

SC   *Sacrosanctum Concilium* (Constitution on the Sacred Liturgy, Vatican II)

SJS   *St. Joseph's Seminary, Dunwoodie, New York, 1896-1921* by Arthur J. Scanlan

TMA   John Paul II, Apostolic Letter. *Tertio Millennio Adveniente*, 10 November 1994

Page 10: PDV §41, 79. **Page 13**: PDV §79, 151. **Page 18**: HJSJ, 18. **Pages 18 and 19**: Excerpts from Bishop John Farley's homily for Dedication Day, cited in HJSJ, pp. 74-87. **Page 21**: PDV §82, 154-155. **Page 22**: DHSJS, 256. **Page 23**: DHSJS, 89. **Page 24**: PDV §42, 82-83. **Page 26**: PDV §60, 114. **Pages 38-39**: SJS, 10, 11, 14, 15, 16, 25, 38, 115. **Page 39**: Lines from Wm. Livingston's poem "The Old Seminary to the New," cited in HJSJ, 118. **Pages 44 and 45**: Excerpts from Father Duffy's article in SJS, 207-209. **Page 46**: PDV §57, 108-109. **Page 48**: PDV §43, 84-85; OT §8, 10-11. **Page 49**: PDV §51, 100; §57, 110. **Page 51**: Cf. Permanent Diaconate Formation Handbook. **Page 53**: AA, §2, 5. **Page 54**: Excerpts from Father Duffy's article in SJS, 212. **Page 55**: DHSJS, 211. **Page 58**: Preface of the Chrism Mass from RM, 413. **Pages 60 and 61**: Research assistance by Trisha McMahon Drain. **Page 62**: Archbishop Ryan cited in HSJS, 62. **Page 70**: From the Solemn Blessing for the Feast of the Epiphany, RM, 571. **Page 73**: TMA, §49, 53. **Page 78**: "Love God's goodness . . . ." from Suzanne Noffke, O.P., ed., *The Letters of St. Catherine of Siena*, vol. 1, Medieval & Renaissance Texts & Studies, vol. 52 (Binghamton, NY 1988), 227. Copyright Arizona Board of Regents for Arizona State University. "Your affections and desires . . . ."; translated by Sr. Mary Jeremiah, O.P., *The Secret of the Heart: A Theological Study of Catherine of Siena's Teaching on the Heart of Jesus*, (Front Royal, VA: Christendom Press, 1995), 99. "Suffering . . . increase[s] . . . .", translated by Suzanne Noffke, O.P., *Catherine of Siena: The Dialogue*, (New York: Paulist Press, 1980), 33. **Page 84**: PDV §38, 74. **Page 86**: PDV §39, 75. **Page 87**: PDV §38, 73. **Page 88**: Consecration of the Chrism, the Chrism Mass, RM, 1018. **Page 89**: The Renewal of Priestly Commitment at the Chrism Mass, RM, 131-132. **Page 92**: From the Exsultet, RM, 181. **Page 95**: From the Exsultet, RM, 175. **Page 97**: From the Exsultet, RM, 175. **Page 99**: Chapel description from HSJS, 111. **Page 100**: From the Exsultet, RM, 175. **Pages 100 and 101**: Source, The History of the Chapel of St. Joseph's Seminary, prepared for the Dedication of the New Altar, 10/16/84. **Pages 102 and 103**: Excerpts from The History of the Organs of Saint Joseph's Seminary by George Hafemann, prepared for the Organ Rededication Ceremony, 12/14/96. **Page 104**: SC §120, 39. **Page 108**: PDV §24, 47. **Page 109**: PDV §79, 151.

Notes for Reverend Avery Dulles' Academic Convocation Address, **Prospects for Seminary Theology**, *delivered 9/17/96*

1. Schlier's 1935 article, "Die Verantwortung der Kirche für den theologischen Unterricht," is discussed by Cardinal Joseph Ratzinger in his *The Nature and Mission of Theology* (San Francisco: Ignatius Press, 1995), 45. **2.** Dietrich Bonhoeffer as quoted by Eberhard Bethge, "The Challenge of Dietrich Bonhoeffer's Life and Theology," *Chicago Theological Seminary Register* 51 (February, 1961); 23. **3.** *Donum veritatis*; English translation in *Origins* 20 (July 5, 1990), 117-26. **4.** John Paul II, Apostolic Exhortation *Pastores dabo vobis* §54; English translation, *I will give you Shepherds* (Boston: St. Paul Books & Media, 1992), 104. **5.** The comprehensive character of theological education is empha- sized by the National Conference of Catholic Bishops in its *Program of Priestly Formation*, fourth edition, November 1992 (Washington, D.C.: United States Catholic Conference, 1993), §§340-342, p. 66. **6.** Ibid., §351, p. 67. **7.** *Pastores dabo vobis*, §42, p. 82. **8.** Ibid., §51, p. 101, quoting from the Synod's *Instrumentum laboris*, 39. **9.** Edward Farley, *Theologia: The Fragmentation and Unity of Theological Education* (Philadelphia: Fortress Press, 1983), 186-187, © 1983 Fortress Press. **10.** Vatican II, Pastoral Constitution *Gaudium et spes*, §15. **11.** This point is well made by David H. Kelsey in his *To Understand God Truly: What's Theological about a Theological School* (Louisville, KY.: Westminister/John Knox, 1992), 173-176 and passim. **12.** *Pastores dabo vobis,* §48, p. 94. **13.** Ibid., §60, p. 114. **14.** I recall this term from his address at Harvard's tercentenary celebration in the spring of 1936. **15.** *Pastores dabo vobis*, §76, p. 146. **16.** On this point see Robert J. Wister, "The Teaching of Theology 1950-90: The American Catholic Experience," *America* 162 (February 3, 1990), 88-109.